MOB

Royal Navy versus the Slave Traders

By the same author

Masters Next to God
They Sank the Red Dragon
The Fighting Tramps
The Grey Widow Maker
Blood and Bushido
SOS - Men Against the Sea
Salvo!
Attack and Sink
Dönitz and the Wold Packs
Return of The Coffin Ships
Beware Raiders!
The Road to Russia
The Quiet Heroes
The Twilight of the U-boats
Beware the Grey Widow Maker
Death in the Doldrums
Japan's Blitzkrieg
War of the U-Boats

Royal Navy versus the Slave Traders

Enforcing Abolition at Sea 1808-1898

Bernard Edwards

Pen & Sword
MARITIME

First published in Great Britain in 2007 by
Pen & Sword Maritime
an imprint of
Pen & Sword Books Ltd
47 Church Street
Barnsley
South Yorkshire
S70 2AS

ISBN 978-1-84415-633-7

A CIP catalogue record for this book is
available from the British Library

Typeset in 11/13 Sabon by
Lamorna Publishing Services

Printed and bound in England by Biddles Ltd

For a complete list of Pen & Sword titles please contact
PEN & SWORD BOOKS LIMITED
47 Church Street, Barnsley, South Yorkshire, S70 2AS, England
E-mail: enquiries@pen-and-sword.co.uk
Website: www.pen-and-sword.co.uk

Thanks to Almighty God and next to the English nation, whose laws relieved us from the bondage in which we have been held.

Robert Peart, Slave, Spanishtown, Jamaica 1838

Author's Note

On 16 March 1807, thanks largely to the persistent efforts of William Wilberforce, Thomas Clarkson and Granville Sharp, the British Parliament passed the Abolition of the Slave Trade Act.

The politicians led the way, but it was left to the men of the Royal Navy's African Squadron to face the guns of the slavers and the killer diseases that haunted the Dark Continent. This they did with exceptional bravery and devotion to duty, standing alone to end an evil that had plagued Africa for so many centuries.

The object of this book is not to re-write history, but to clear away the fog of accusations and recriminations that surround the slave trade.

The author wishes to thank Africa Christian Action of Claremont, South Africa for its generous help in obtaining illustrations for this book.

Contents

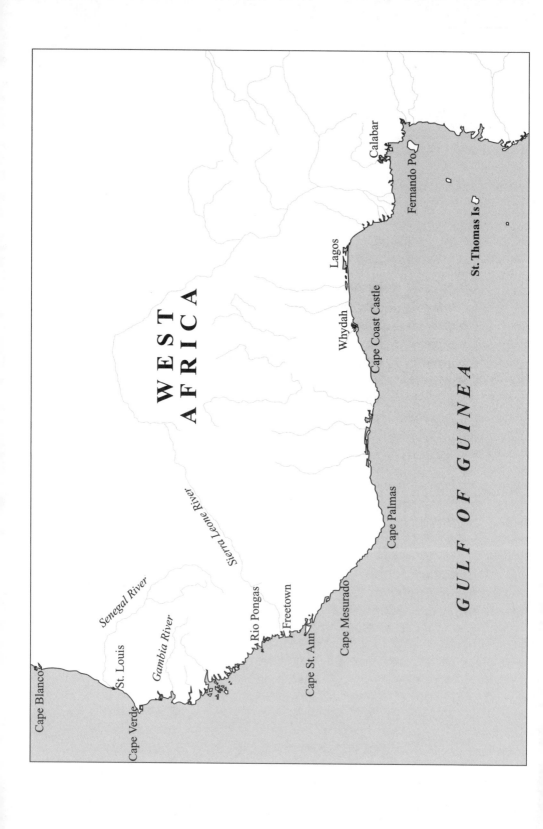

WEST
AFRICA

Senegal River

Gambia River

Sierra Leone River

Rio Pongas

Freetown

Cape Blanco

St. Louis

Cape Verde

Cape St. Ann

Cape Mesurado

Cape Palmas

Cape Coast Castle

Whydah

Lagos

Calabar

Fernando Po

St. Thomas Is

GULF OF GUINEA

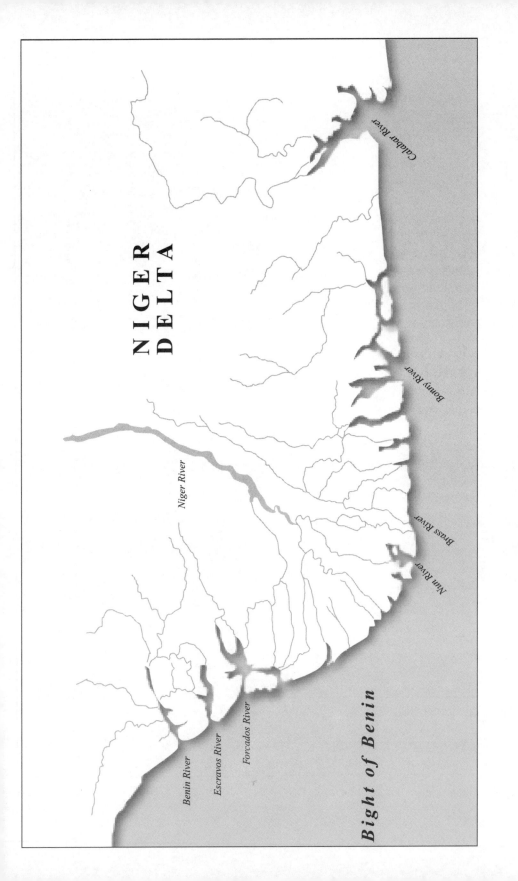

NIGER DELTA

Niger River

Benin River

Escravos River

Forcados River

Nun River

Brass River

Bonny River

Calabar River

Bight of Benin

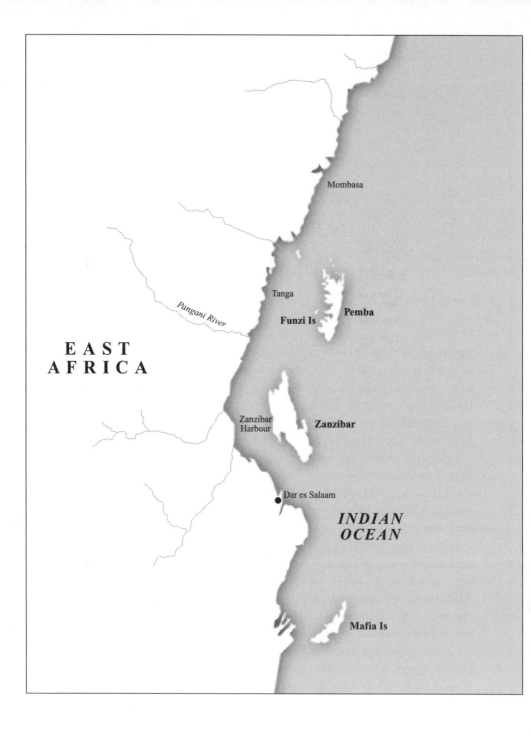

Mombasa

Tanga

Pangani River

Funzi Is

Pemba

**E A S T
A F R I C A**

Zanzibar
Harbour

Zanzibar

Dar es Salaam

*INDIAN
OCEAN*

Mafia Is

Chapter One

A Family Trait

When, lo, out of the darkness there was light,
There in the sea were England and her ships.

John Masefield

In the gathering dusk of 5 November 1940 Convoy HX 84 was in mid-Atlantic, and had reached the point of no return in its eastbound passage. The comparative safety of American waters lay far astern, and ahead, nearly a thousand miles over the horizon, was Fortress Britain, ringed by marauding U-boats, and beckoning urgently. For HX 84 there was no turning back.

Steaming closed up in nine columns abreast, the thirty-seven deep-loaded merchantmen forming the convoy were enjoying a spell of rare good weather for the time of the year. The normally turbulent ocean was quiescent, the sky showing patches of blue, and the horizon was as sharp as a whetted knife. For the men manning the open bridges of the merchant ships, balaclava-red and duffel-coated against the cold of the approaching night, this was a welcome relief from the usual savagery of the North Atlantic in winter, and they were savouring it to the full. But to the man ultimately responsible for their safety the unnatural calm spelled danger.

Captain Edward Fogarty Fegen, RN, commanding HX 84's sole escort vessel, the armed merchant cruiser *Jervis Bay*, had good reason to be ill at ease. His ageing ex-passenger liner command, armed with seven obsolete 5.9s firing over open sights, was all that stood between HX 84 and the hordes of a determined enemy. On that day, Fogarty Fegen would have sold his soul for the cover of a roaring Atlantic gale.

1

And as the last of the daylight faded, Fegen's worst fears were realised. Over the horizon came the German pocket-battleship *Admiral Scheer*, her director-controlled 11-inch gun turrets belching smoke and flame.

The 12,000-ton *Admiral Scheer* was one of Hitler's powerful *Panzerschiff* class, built specifically to hunt down and destroy British merchant shipping. She was armed with eight 5.9-inch and six 11-inch guns – the finest Krupps could supply – she had a top speed of 26½ knots, and a cruising range of 19,000 miles without refuelling. Under the command of *Kapitän-zur-See* Theodor Krancke, the *Admiral Scheer* had left the Baltic on 24 October, and three days later slipped through the Denmark Strait into the North Atlantic undetected. Krancke's orders were to mount an attack on British convoys in the North Atlantic, which at this time were said to be only lightly escorted due to the withdrawal of many of the Royal Navy's ships to the Mediterranean following the Italian declaration of war. HX 84 was to be Krancke's first target.

For the *Jervis Bay* the odds seemed insurmountable, but Edward Stephen Fogarty Fegen, descended from the Irish kings, son of an admiral, and nurtured in the fires of the Great War of 1914-18, recognised only one answer to the danger threatening. Ordering the convoy to scatter, he sent his men to their action stations, and steamed straight for the *Admiral Scheer*, his 5.9s spitting defiance.

What followed was predictable. The German guns outranged those of the *Jervis Bay* by nearly 7000 yards, and the slow, high-sided British auxiliary was on fire and crippled long before she came close enough to land a shell on the *Admiral Scheer*. Forty-nine-year-old Captain Edward Fogarty Fegen died on the bridge of his ship with his face to the enemy.

The hero of the *Jervis Bay* was only four years old when in May 1887 his father, Frederick Fogarty Fegen, was serving as a lieutenant in the screw corvette HMS *Turquoise*, one of the slave-hunters of the Royal Navy's African Squadron. The *Turquoise*, armed with twelve 64-pounder muzzle-loading rifles, had been assigned to patrol the east coast of Africa in the region of Zanzibar, where Arab slave traders were known to be active.

On 28 May, when the *Turquoise* was cruising between Zanzibar and the neighbouring island of Pemba, Lieutenant Fogarty Fegen was sent away in the corvette's steam pinnace with a crew of eight and an Arab interpreter. His orders were to intercept, board and search any Arab slaving dhows attempting to break out into the Indian Ocean by sailing north of Pemba. It was after sunset when the pinnace reached the Fundu Gap, a navigable channel favoured by the dhows between Pemba's small satellite islands of Fundu and Njao. Fegen brought the pinnace to an anchor off the entrance to the Gap, and settled down to wait out the night.

The hours of darkness passed slowly and uncomfortably. The air was hot and humid, and a heavy swell coming in from seaward had the shallow draught pinnace rolling her gunwales under. Sleep was impossible, and the dawn could not come quickly enough for Fegen and his men.

Punctually as ever, the tropical sun climbed over the horizon at 6 am, bringing with it the first dhow heading out to sea through the Fundu Gap, her single triangular sail bellying in the early morning off-shore breeze. She was obviously heavily loaded, and might well be a legitimate trader with a cargo of cloves for Arabia. However, after studying her through the long glass, Fegen came to the conclusion that she was more likely to be a slaver bound for the Persian Gulf with a human cargo. He decided to investigate.

The pinnace's small dinghy was lowered and, manned by Frederick Russell, *Turquoise*'s captain of the maintop, Able Seaman Frederick Blanchard and an Arab interpreter, set off to intercept the dhow. Meanwhile, the pinnace, her 9-pounder gun manned and her remaining crew armed with rifles and cutlasses, stood by to give support if needed. Not that Lieutenant Fegen anticipated any serious resistance, and in any case, in his opinion it was most unlikely that the Arabs would be armed with anything more lethal than a few old flintlock muskets and rusty swords.

When the dinghy was within 100 yards of the dhow, Frederick Russell stood up in the bows and hailed her. There was no reply, and neither did the dhow shorten sail. Her deck appeared to be empty, except for the shadowy figure of a lone man at her tiller.

Russell's second challenge also produced no response and, being well experienced in boarding suspect slavers, the petty officer's suspicions were thoroughly aroused. He challenged again, and this time his shout was answered by a fusillade of rifle shots fired by unseen marksmen in the dhow.

Instinctively ducking to avoid the bullets whistling all around him, Russell lost his balance and fell overboard. Blanchard returned the fire with his revolver, but this prompted another hail of bullets from the Arab craft, forcing him and the interpreter to take cover in the bottom of the boat. Russell, who had meanwhile been attempting to reboard the dinghy, dropped back and swam clear, followed by another hail of bullets kicking up the water at his heels like angry hailstones.

Seeing the dire plight of his boarding party, Lieutenant Fegen brought the pinnace in at full speed, aiming to put her between the Arab dhow and the dinghy. This he succeeded in doing, but to his horror saw the dhow heel over under full helm and head straight for his pinnace, with the obvious intent of ramming. The dhow had the wind right astern and closed the gap between the two craft so fast that Fegen had no time to take avoiding action.

The dhow slammed into the pinnace's starboard side near her bow, and the two vessels, their rigging entangled, swung broadside on to each other. Immediately their gunwales touched, a horde of screaming Arabs, armed with modern rifles and gleaming swords, rose up from behind the dhow's bulwarks and attempted to swarm aboard the British pinnace.

Calling on his men to repel boarders, Fegen, revolver in one hand and cutlass in the other, shot the first Arab boarder and ran the next one through. Marine James Blyth, fighting shoulder to shoulder with the lieutenant, went down with a bullet in his thigh from a ricochet off the mast but, although he was bleeding profusely, continued to return the enemy's fire until he lost consciousness.

Able Seaman Thomas Hall, meanwhile, was engaged in a desperate hand-to-hand fight with another Arab. Hall's cutlass was knocked from his hand, but he fought on, using a broken boat hook as a club, until his opponent retreated to the safety of his own deck. By now, Hall's fighting spirit was fully aroused, and he was about to follow when he caught sight of a rifle barrel poking through a gap in the dhow's bulwarks, aimed at Marine Blyth, who was lying helpless on the pinnace's deck. With total

4

disregard for his own safety, Hall lunged forward, knocked up the rifle, and for his pains took a bullet through his left hand when the gun went off.

Frederick Russell, dripping water, had by now clambered back aboard the dinghy, and with Able Seaman Blanchard was directing a fierce fire at the undefended port side of the dhow. When they realised what was happening, the Arabs fired back, and Russell went down screaming with pain having taken a bullet in his ankle. Blanchard continued firing, taking what little cover he could find behind the dinghy's gunwale.

Being under attack from both sides did not deter the Arabs, who it could now be seen were at least twenty or thirty strong, and they continued their efforts to board the pinnace. Lieutenant Fegen soon found himself isolated from his crew, and surrounded by ferocious Arabs intent on killing him. His revolver empty, Fegen put his back to the mast and prepared to sell his life dearly, wielding his short Navy cutlass against half a dozen two-handed swords. A blade cut deep into his right arm, the cutlass flew from his hand, and he would have been hacked to death had it not been for the timely interference of Able Seaman John Pearson. Broad in the shoulder, as strong as an ox and totally without fear, Pearson charged the Arabs, whirling his cutlass and hurling abuse in colourful seaman's language. He decapitated one man and forced the other attackers to beat a hasty retreat in the face of his assault.

Although Arab dead and wounded now littered the deck of the pinnace, the British seamen were still heavily outnumbered and in imminent danger of being overwhelmed. Then a sudden gust of wind saved them. The dhow began to break away from the pinnace, and seeing they were about to be isolated on the enemy's deck, the surviving Arabs lost all stomach for the fight. They scrambled back aboard the dhow which, with its sail billowing in the strengthening wind, drew slowly away.

Fegen was on his feet again and, determined to press home the advantage, rallied his crew and set off in pursuit. But no matter how furiously the pinnace's boiler furnace was stoked, she was unable to close the gap between the two craft. The 9-pounder gun in the bows was manned, but before it could be fired a well-aimed – or perhaps lucky – rifle shot killed the dhow's helmsman. With no one at her tiller, the dhow broached to in the swell, and ran headlong on to the shelving beach of Njao Island.

Now, for the first time, Fegen's earlier assessment of the dhow's cargo was confirmed. Those Arabs who were still alive threw themselves over the side into the surf, to be closely followed by a howling tide of black humanity. The water was shallow, but Fegen brought his pinnace in as close to the wreck as possible to rescue fifty-three terrified Africans who were destined for slavery. Many others were drowned in the surf.

When the stranded dhow was boarded, nine Arabs were found lying dead on her bloodstained deck. The rest of the slaver's crew had reached the shore and disappeared into the interior. Mustering his own crew, Fegen was relieved to find them all alive. Five, including himself, had been wounded, the most seriously hurt being Frederick Russell, with a bullet in his foot, and Able Seaman Benjamin Stone, who had been shot in the leg. Both these wounds required urgent medical attention.

Turquoise was nowhere in sight, having continued on her patrol, and with fifty-three extra souls on board the pinnace was too overloaded to put out to sea. Fegen had no alternative but to land the rescued slaves, leaving them to fend for themselves. This done, he set sail for Funzi Island, which lies off the west coast of Pemba, where there was an unmanned naval depot. On anchoring off Funzi, the dinghy was sent to Zanzibar to get help.

Eleven days elapsed before HMS *Reindeer*, which had a doctor on board, arrived at the anchorage. In the meantime, Frederick Russell's foot had been saved by the application of poultices made from crushed ship's biscuits. But there was no saving Ben Stone. Gangrene had set in, and although *Reindeer*'s doctor amputated his leg, Stone died of his wounds. He was buried on Funzi.

In recognition of his initiative and leadership in this action Lieutenant Frederick Fogarty Fegen was promoted to commander. He went on to reach the rank of vice-admiral in 1910, by which time his son, Edward Fogarty Fegen, later to command the *Jervis Bay*, was serving as a midshipman in the Royal Navy.

Able Seaman Benjamin Stone was one of the last men of the African Squadron to lay down his life to end the evil that was the African slave trade. This thankless battle fought by the Squadron had been long and hard, always with too few ships, too few men, and tremendous obstacles to overcome. At times, it seemed that every man's hand – black and white – was turned against them. Added to this were the clammy, overpowering heat, the debilitating diseases, and the sheer, soul-destroying boredom of the long patrols. That this gallant little band who formed the Royal Navy's African Squadron, often fighting alone, defeated a heinous trade which had flourished for so many centuries, was little short of a miracle. Sadly, largely because of the efforts of those who take such great delight in belittling the achievements of their own nation, the work of the British African Squadron has so far received scant recognition.

Chapter Two

The Beginning

Those sold by the Blacks are for the most part prisoners of war, taken either in fight, or pursuit, or in the incursions they make into their enemies' territories; others stolen away by their own countrymen; and some there are, who will sell their own children, kindred, or neighbours.

John Bardot, Agent, French Royal African Company

Contrary to popular belief, slavery in Africa was not initiated by the white man but was home grown, often the consequence of inter-tribal warfare. Long before the arrival of foreigners on their shores, it was the habit of local chieftains to make slaves of prisoners taken in battle. Any surviving men, women and children on the losing side were enslaved as a matter of course and for as long as their conquerors wished. In the rare times when peace reigned between the tribes, the shortfall was made up by enslaving those who committed crimes against the community. However, this form of slavery was often only superficial, life in the African hinterland then being largely a matter of existing from day to day. Slaves were rarely ill treated or seriously confined, and it is doubtful whether any of those taken were much, if at all, worse off than they had been before. All that changed when the Arabs came.

In the 9th century AD, the cycle of world domination was in the hands of the Arabs who, on the pretext of finding converts for Islam, had emerged from their desert peninsula beyond the Red Sea, and swept westwards to conquer the southern shores of the Mediterranean and much of Spain. A proud, arrogant people, the Arabs found manual work demeaning, and were delighted when they discovered a vast untapped pool of labour in the lush forests of Equatorial Africa south of the Sahara. Here were people who were simple and unworldly to the point of naivety. Cut off from the rest of the world, cocooned in their dark, fetish-ridden jungles, where food was in abundance, and the minimum of effort was required to sustain life, for them time had stood still for thousands of years. They were well and truly stuck in the Stone Age, their only attribute being their great physical strength. This and their simplistic outlook on life made them ripe for exploitation.

When the Arabs came bearing exotic gifts – in reality worthless trinkets – it took little persuasion for African kings and chiefs to hand over their surplus slaves. Soon regular caravans of black captives were wending their painful way north to the Arab cities on the shores of the Mediterranean and across the Sudan to the desert sands of Arabia. This enforced migration sometimes reached as many as 10,000 slaves a year, by which the African rulers prospered, and the demands of the Arab households were satisfied. It is on record that, although the Arabs had little regard for their black captives, rating them marginally above the beasts of the forest, and driving them without mercy when on the march, once on Arab soil they did not treat them badly. Should any slave chose to convert to Islam, then, in theory at least, he became the equal of his master in the eyes of God. Furthermore, the Koran offered immortality to any true believer who in his lifetime had set a slave free. In consequence, many ex-slaves found themselves free men in a foreign land far from home. The apparent magnanimity of Islam proved to be a mixed blessing. Abandoned by their erstwhile masters, freed slaves had no other means of support, and with no hope of returning to their native shores, remained slaves in all but name.

Centuries after the Arabs, the Europeans came on the scene. In 1394, Philippa, wife of John I, King of Portugal, and daughter of John of Gaunt, Duke of Lancaster, gave birth to a son, Henry. This was an event that was to change the face of the world. From an early age, Prince Henry took a keen interest in ships and the sea, and evinced an insatiable desire to know what lay beyond the horizon. This was at a time when the popular belief in Europe was that the earth was flat, and to venture out of sight of land

9

was to court disaster. By the time he was in his twenties, Henry's enthusiasm for exploration had led him to set up an observatory and school of navigation at Cape Sagres, on the coast of the Algarve. There Henry the Navigator, as he had become known, gathered around him an elite circle of mathematicians, cartographers, astronomers and shipwrights, the cream of the Mediterranean's specialists in exploration planning.

Henry had a dream – to push the bounds of Portuguese discovery beyond Cape Bojador, then further south than any European ship had yet sailed. Beyond Bojador, a barren headland on the Atlantic coast of the Sahara, some 800 miles south-south-west of Sagres, lay – or so it was said – the abode of the Devil himself, where the heat of the sun was so fierce that the sea boiled, and men were roasted alive. No white man had ever ventured past Cape Bojador and returned to tell the tale. It was this myth – and he regarded it as such – that Henry the Navigator was determined to dispel, and further, he vowed to send ships south to find the way around Africa to the fabled land of Cathay in the east. His first priority was to build a fleet of ships capable of the long and potentially hazardous ocean voyage.

At that time, trade in Mediterranean waters was carried mainly by *barcas*, small, clumsy two-masted vessels rigged with lateen sails. These craft, designed mainly for inshore fishing, had great difficulty in making forward progress unless the wind was well abaft the beam, and they were totally unsuited to the rigours of the open Atlantic. Henry's first challenge to his team of experts was to produce something better. The result was the three-masted *caravela*, square-rigged on the two forward masts, and lateen-rigged on the mizzen. Averaging 80 feet in length and around 70 tons burthen, the *caravelas* had an axled rudder and, most importantly, were capable of tacking into the wind. Prince Henry's new ships were the finest ever seen in European waters, and the forerunners of a new era in sail.

The continued efforts of the wise men of Sagres also produced the finest charts ever seen – albeit still largely a matter of guesswork beyond Cape Bojador – a new concept in navigational instruments, and a select band of mariners to crew the new ships. The outstanding individual was a young Portuguese captain named Gil Eannes, who Henry duly sent south to break through the barrier of fear and fantasy posed by Bojador. Eannes and his crew, as they prepared to challenge the unknown, might truly be likened to the first astronauts to go into space some 500 years later.

Gil Eannes rounded Cape Bojador early in the year 1433, and to his great surprise – and relief – sailed not into a sea of liquid flame, but into waters that were little different from those to the north. The weather was hot and humid, but the notorious cape turned out to be a low, red-sand headland posing no more of a threat to the mariner than a few breaking reefs offshore. After a brief exploration of the area, Eannes hurried back to Sagres with news of his discovery.

Within two years of Gil Eannes' memorable voyage, Prince Henry's navigators had sailed 120 miles beyond Cape Bojador, and in 1441 Antão Gonçalves, Chamberlain to the Prince, landed on the West African coast near the Rio de Oro, 150 miles south of Bojador. Gonçalves returned with a cargo of valuable skins, salt, gold dust, and ten Negroes he claimed had been presented to him by an Arab mounted on a white camel. At this time Portugal was in the grip of an acute shortage of manual labour, brought about by the scourge of the Black Death, and the potential of the Negroes, who were physically strong, was quickly realized. More were demanded. Three years later, Lançarote de Freitas, a pupil of Henry the Navigator, came back with a cargo of 235 Negroes from Senegal. This constituted the first major import of African slaves into Europe.

The fear of the unknown beyond Cape Bojador being dispelled, other Portuguese sea captains ventured further and further south, reaching the river kingdom of Gambia and on into the Gulf of Guinea. Local chiefs, dazzled by the offer of horses, silks and silver, enthusiastically rounded up their surplus subjects and handed them over into slavery. The Portuguese, like the Arabs before them, sincerely believed they were saving the souls of these poor blacks and offering them a far better life than they had enjoyed in their own Godless land. The latter may have been true, but the numbers involved were never great, reaching barely a thousand a year by 1448. And so the traffic in African slaves, repugnant though it may have seemed to some, promised to remain within reasonable bounds, and only in the hands of the

11

Portuguese and Arabs, both convinced they were carrying out God's work. Then Europe developed a sweet tooth.

In the 15th century, the European diet was almost totally devoid of any sweetening agent except honey, a delicacy not easy to come by. Sugar, first grown in India as early as 327 BC, was largely unknown in Europe. Some sugar canes had been brought from the East by the Moors and were cultivated in the far south of Spain, but the harvest was minute, ensuring that sugar was beyond the reach of all but the very rich. Once again, it was the entrepreneurial Prince Henry of Portugal who led the way, introducing sugar cane into his new colony of Madeira. The temperate climate of this Atlantic island was well suited to the cultivation of the cane, and it flourished, although by virtue of Madeira's size the crop was again limited. It was not until the Spaniards carried sugar cane plants to the islands of the Caribbean, and the Portuguese opened up extensive plantations in Brazil, that sugar became a widely traded commodity.

Able for the first time to lay their hands on sugar in quantity, Europeans quickly became addicted to this remarkable source of energy, which perhaps had very much the same effect on a body unused to it as some of the stimulant drugs of today. They just could not get enough of the sweet substance, and it was not long before the plantations of the West Indies and Brazil ran into an acute shortage of field workers. The harvesting of sugar cane in the tropical heat was back-breaking work, to which the indigenous population of these colonies – largely poor whites and ex-prisoners from Iberia – was totally unsuited. Forced to work on the plantations by their Spanish and Portuguese masters, they succumbed to exhaustion and disease at an alarming rate. Those who survived eventually took to the hills, and the need to import foreign labour became urgent. Surprisingly, it was a Spanish missionary, Bishop Bartolome de Las Casas, who offered a solution to the sugar growers' dilemma. Las Casas, who had spent a lifetime campaigning against the enslavement of the Indians in Hispaniola, recommended that Negroes be imported from West Africa to work in the fields. He justified his recommendation with the proviso that these 'savages' be baptised into the Christian Church and thus rescued from their heathen state. Yet again, whether he was in agreement or not, the African was being saved from himself.

And so began the transatlantic slave trade, an infamous trade that might well have remained exclusively in the hands of Spain and Portugal, had it not been for an unfortunate experience suffered by the English merchant venturer John Hawkins.

From the beginning of the 16th century England, mainly through the efforts of Henry VIII, had begun to challenge Spain and Portugal for the supremacy of the seas, and thus for access to the immense riches to be found in far lands. Up until that time, much of the New World had been considered the province of Spain and Portugal alone. In 1445 Pope Alexander VI issued a papal bull granting Spain autonomy over all land and sea to the west of Europe, while Portugal was given free rein to exploit the East. England, being regarded as an abode of barbarians – Henry had broken away from the Catholic Church when Pope Clement VII refused to grant him a divorce from Catherine of Aragon – was left out in the cold.

Captain, later Sir John, Hawkins enjoyed the patronage of Queen Elizabeth, who in 1562 put one of her ships, the *Jesus of Lubeck*, at his disposal. Financed by the Earls of Leicester and Pembroke, Hawkins made two successful voyages to the West Indies carrying slaves from West Africa. These he sold to the Spanish colonists, who appeared not to object to the Englishman encroaching on what was traditionally considered to be their trade. Hawkins then assumed he was free to build on the enterprise, and on his third voyage he was accompanied by his soon-to-be famous cousin Francis Drake, then sailing in the *Minion*. Meeting with heavy weather on the passage from West Africa, Hawkins and Drake put into the Mexican port of San Juan de Ulloa to make repairs. The local Spaniards at first welcomed them, but when they realized the English ships were slavers, they opened fire on them with their shore batteries. The *Jesus of Lubeck* was sunk but Hawkins was rescued by the *Minion*. The two cousins sailed away from the Caribbean determined to come back with more slaves and also, in due course, to take their revenge on the treacherous Spaniards.

Whilst the exploits of John Hawkins and other Elizabethan sea-rovers may have been the beginning of British involvement in the transatlantic slave trade, it was not until a hundred years later that this became a serious enterprise. In 1627, when Elizabeth was long dead and the ill-fated Charles I was on the throne, the first sugar plantations were set up on Barbados. By the middle of the 18th century, there were some 1,500 such plantations in the British West Indies, for which a large and continuous supply of labour was needed. Within a few years around 200 British ships were employed full-time carrying slaves from West Africa, not only to the West Indies, but to the Spanish and Portuguese colonies in the Americas. In fact, nearly fifty per cent of slaves crossing the Atlantic were by then being carried in British bottoms. The British, as always, had been slow to grasp the opportunity, but when they did, with characteristic daring and determination, they showed that they were the best in the business. And they were never short of cargoes to carry. Prisoners of war taken in deliberately engineered tribal wars provided a ready supply. When no excuse could be found to attack their neighbours, African chiefs resorted to more subtle methods of supplying the needs of the slave traders. Criminal offences punishable by sale into bondage multiplied, and royal wives caught in adultery were liable to the same punishment. In the latter case, it became very profitable for a chief to marry dozens of young girls, leave them to their own devices, and count on their natural urges to lead them into adultery. When all else failed, the monarchs were known to accuse their own subjects of plotting to overthrow them, thereby furnishing an excuse to seize and sell on the 'plotters'.

Typical of British ships then engaged in the slave trade was the 150-ton snow *Zong*, owned by the Liverpool merchants William Gregson and George Case. She was an 85ft long three-master, square-rigged on both fore and mainmast and with a fore and aft trysail abaft the mizzen. With this rig she was easy to handle and carried a crew of only fourteen men, a hallmark of the trade in which she was engaged, the transport of slaves.

It was soon after dawn on 6 September 1781, with the night mist still shrouding the wooded valleys of the island, when the *Zong* eased away from St. Thomas, in the Bight of Biafra, her sails barely drawing in the light off-shore breeze. Although the sun was not yet above the horizon, the day was already hot and oppressive. Aft, on the *Zong*'s poop deck, her master, Captain

Luke Collingwood, his thin cotton shirt already showing dark patches of sweat, leaned on the taffrail and gazed wistfully astern at the land he was leaving.

St. Thomas Island – São Tomé to its Portuguese colonisers – lying 170 miles off the mainland with the Equator running through its southernmost point, was not the usual West African cesspit, dank, fetid and disease-ridden. On the contrary, by some climatic quirk, this was an island paradise, the tip of its 6000-ft sleeping volcano covered with snow most of the year, and its hillsides and deep valleys thick with sweet-scented lemon trees. The well-watered soil produced an abundance of fruit and vegetables, pigs and goats thrived in the flatlands, and coveys of wild turkeys and partridges flitted through the undergrowth. Also blessed with sparkling streams of clear, cool water tumbling down its mountainsides, St. Thomas was the ideal stopping-off place for ships like the *Zong*, about to set off on the long Atlantic crossing – the notorious Middle Passage.

With a sigh, Collingwood turned to face the bows, and as he did so breathed in the overpowering stench of his cargo. Crammed into the *Zong*'s single hold were no fewer than 442 African slaves, labour destined for the plantations of Jamaica and certain to yield a fat profit for William Gregson and George Case, both much respected ex-mayors of the City of Liverpool.

Luke Collingwood had loaded his human cargo in the fever-ridden estuaries in the north of the Bight of Benin and, as was the custom of the trade, coasted down on the south-easterly flowing Guinea Current to St. Thomas to reprovision. Baskets of fresh vegetables, a few live goats, and well-filled water butts worked wonders to boost the morale of his crew, already low at the prospect of the long and difficult passage across the ocean. The full water butts were particularly necessary for, at the very least, the *Zong* might expect to be at sea for five to six weeks. If the winds were contrary, and this so often was the case, then three months might elapse before they made land in the West Indies. Whatever came to pass, with 458 humans crammed into a ship only 85 feet long and 25 feet in the beam, the 5000-mile voyage promised to be an ordeal few would willingly undertake. For Collingwood and his crew success would bring handsome rewards; for the slaves who survived the horrors of the long sea

15

passage, ahead lay only the prospect of a lifetime's forced labour.

The voyage started well, for once clear of St. Thomas the *Zong* picked up the south-east trades and, with the wind astern, for the next two weeks bowled along at a cracking pace on a north-westerly course. Then, as Luke Collingwood knew full well she would, she ran into the Doldrums, the broad band of calms and light variable winds that straddles the Equator. This was the nightmare described so eloquently by Coleridge's Ancient Mariner. For day after day, her sails hanging limp and her decks bleaching white in the hot sun, the *Zong* drifted aimlessly, her only progress to the west being a dozen or so miles a day with the aid of the south-equatorial current. Six weeks passed with agonising slowness, before she broke free of the calms and the first of the north-east trades began to fill her sails.

Soon the lonely Atlantic sentinels of St. Paul's Rocks were in sight, and with the *Zong* running free on the starboard tack, Luke Collingwood edged in towards the coast of Brazil. He was seeking to catch the flow of the south-equatorial current again, which would provide another half knot to help carry him into the Caribbean. Time was now of the essence, for after nearly two months at sea conditions on board the slaver were rapidly deteriorating. Food was short – down to a diet of rancid salt beef and weevily biscuits for the crew, while the slaves had to make do with a mash of ground cassava root, and little of it. What fresh water remained in the butts was foul with green slime, and almost undrinkable.

Not surprisingly, sickness broke out amongst the poor African wretches packed in the stifling heat of the hold. Then they began to die, some from the dreadful tropical diseases brought with them from the jungle, others from melancholy brought on by the sheer hopelessness of their plight. In all, in the space of a few weeks, sixty slaves died and found lonely graves in the vast ocean. They were eventually joined by seven of Collingwood's crew. The sharks following in the wake of the *Zong* were well fed.

As he coaxed his ship towards the West Indies, Collingwood was aware of yet another danger threatening, this being the tail end of the hurricane season in this part of the ocean. Originating in mid-Atlantic in around 10 degrees north latitude, these destructive storms track west-north-westwards towards the West

Indies, usually re-curving to the north in about latitude 30 degrees, but sometimes sweeping across the islands and into the Caribbean. Should she be unfortunate enough to be caught up in one of these demonstrations of nature at its angriest, the little *Zong* could well find herself fighting for her life in winds of up to 100 knots and mountainous seas. In open waters, she would have room to run away from the danger, but once in the Caribbean her ability to manoeuvre would be severely curtailed, with perhaps disastrous consequences.

Captain Collingwood's fears for the weather came to naught. The *Zong* passed to the south of the Windward Islands on 18 November and entered the Caribbean with fair winds and blue skies. Nine days later, on the 27th, land was again sighted, which should have been the eastern end of Jamaica. However, for reasons known only to himself, Luke Collingwood insisted that it must be the southern tip of the island of Hispaniola, some 270 miles further east. The *Zong*'s first mate, James Kelsal, challenged Collingwood's navigation, but by this time a hurricane really was in the offing, and both men had other things to occupy them. To avoid the storm Collingwood decided to run to leeward, away from the land.

By this time the situation on board the British ship was desperate. Her water supply was running dangerously low, with the result that Collingwood was forced to cut the ration to the bare minimum necessary to sustain life. The white men survived, but for the poor wretches confined to their crowded prison below decks this was the ultimate deprivation. The daily death toll rose rapidly.

The success of this voyage depended on delivering the slaves alive and well to the market in Jamaica, and Luke Collingwood could see his owners' profit rapidly disappearing. With it would go the generous reward he stood to receive for the successful completion of the voyage. He decided to take steps to remedy the worsening situation.

Under British maritime law, it was then, and still is now, legitimate in a dire emergency to throw cargo overboard in order to save the vessel. This is deemed 'jetsam', and any loss may be charged to the insurers. On the basis of this law Collingwood reasoned that although he had only live slaves in the hold, they

17

could be classed as 'cargo'. He consulted with his officers, and in spite of the protests of James Kelsal it was agreed that any slave that was sick and unlikely to complete the voyage should be jettisoned. On 29 November fifty-two slaves were brought up from the hold and thrown overboard. Forty-two followed the next day, and although it had rained in the meantime and there was no shortage of water on board, on 1 December another twenty-six poor black souls were dragged to the rail and pitched over the side. Soon after that, ten more, despairing of their plight, cheated Collingwood and threw themselves overboard.

When the *Zong* returned to Liverpool, her owners claimed on their insurance for the loss of the slaves, and it seems that their claim might have been met in full, had details of Captain Luke Collingwood's inhuman conduct not leaked out. Much to the dismay of William Gregson and George Case, the case then went to court.

In July 1783, the anti-slavery campaigner Granville Sharp wrote a report of the incident for the Prime Minister and the Lords of the Admiralty, in which he said:

The sickness and mortality on board the *Zong* previous to 29 November (the time when they began to throw the poor negroes overboard alive), was not occasioned by the want of water; for it was proved that they did not discover till that very next day, the 29 November (or the preceding day) that the stock of fresh water was reduced to 200 gallons: yet the same day, or in the evening of it, before any soul had been put to short allowance, and before there was any present or real want of water, the master of the ship called together a few of the officers and told them of the following effect – that if the slaves died a natural death, it would be a loss to the owners of the ship; but if they were thrown alive into the sea, it would be a loss of the underwriters: and to palliate the inhuman proposal he, the said Collingwood, pretended that 'it would not be so cruel to throw the poor sick wretches (meaning such slaves) into the sea, as to suffer them to linger out a few days under the disorders with which they were afflicted,' or expressed himself to the like effect. To which proposal the mate (whose name is Colonel James Kelsal) objected, it seems,

18

at first, and said there was 'no present want of water to justify such a measure.' But the said Luke Collingwood prevailed upon the crew, or the rest of them, to listen to his said proposal, and the same evening, and two or three of some few following days, the said Luke Collingwood picked, or caused to be picked out, from the cargo of the same ship 133 slaves, all or most of whom were sick or weak, and not likely to live; and ordered the crew by turns to throw them into the sea; which most inhuman order was cruelly complied with. I am informed by a memorandum from the deposition of Kelsal, the chief mate (one of the murderers), that fifty-four persons were actually thrown overboard alive on 29 November, and that forty-two more were also thrown overboard on 1 December. And on this very day, 1 December 1781, before the stock of water was consumed, here fell a plentiful rain, which by confession of one of their own advocates, 'continued a day or two, and enabled them to collect six casks of water, which was full allowance for eleven days, or for twenty-three days at half allowance,' whereas the ship actually arrived at Jamaica in twenty-one days afterwards – viz on 22 December 1781. They seem also to have had an opportunity of sending a boat for water no less than thirteen days sooner, viz on 19 December, when they 'made the west end of Jamaica distant two or three leagues only,' as I am informed by a person who was on board... .

There can be little doubt that Luke Collingwood and his crew committed murder on the high seas with the object of protecting the investment of their employers. And yet, when the case came before the courts in London, the defence was offered that the slaves had been thrown overboard in order to save the ship and those remaining alive on board, just as might be done with items of cargo to lighten a ship sinking in a storm. Collingwood was dead by the time the case was heard, but his actions were proved to be legal. The barrister acting for the owners of the *Zong* argued: 'So far from a charge of murder lying against these people, there is not the least imputation – of cruelty, I will not say – but (even) of propriety.' The barrister's plea was accepted by the Lord Chief Justice, Lord Mansfield, who commented there was 'no doubt, though it shocks one very much, that the case of the slaves was the same as if horses had been thrown overboard.' In due course, those stalwart burghers of the City of Liverpool, William Gregson and George Case, received payment from the underwriters amounting to £30 for each slave thrown overboard to 'save the ship.'

It later came to light that at the time the first slaves were thrown overboard from the *Zong* there was no shortage of drinking water on board. In fact, the ship is said to have arrived in Jamaica on 22 December with 420 gallons to spare. If this was the case, then Luke Collingwood can have had no other motive for jettisoning his slaves other than to protect his owners' interests. Had justice prevailed, then Collingwood and the members of his crew involved must surely have been found guilty of murder. They were not, but some good did come of this sordid business, in that the publicity generated by the *Zong* case provided valuable ammunition for that small band of concerned men in Britain who were campaigning for the abolition of slavery.

Chapter Three

The British Slavers

That such a system should so long have been suffered to exist in any part of the British Empire will appear to our posterity almost incredible.

William Wilberforce

The *Zong* case was heard in 1783, three hundred and forty-two years after Antão Gonçalves had proudly paraded his string of African captives before Prince Henry of Portugal, and by which time the transatlantic slave trade was reaching its apogee. What had begun as a novel experiment had become a growth industry, with as many as 80,000 men, women and children being ferried across the Atlantic every year, supplying labour for the booming plantations of the West Indies and the American mainland. Spain, Portugal, Britain, America, France, Denmark, Sweden and the Netherlands were all involved in this extremely lucrative enterprise. More than half the trade was being carried in British slavers, proving once again – and this time to their eternal shame – that when the British concentrate their minds on a project, they are more than a match for any competitors. In this case, the incentive was Britain's rapidly expanding empire in the Americas, there being a desperate need for cheap labour in these colonies.

With the passage of time, the ships used to transport slaves had progressed from the small, single-decked caravels of Prince Henry's day to purpose-built slavers, or guinea-men, as they were known, brigs or snows of around 150 tons burthen. By modern standards these were tiny ships, comparable in size to a North Sea trawler, yet they crammed in as many as 500 slaves below decks, and on voyages that were measured in months rather than weeks.

21

The guinea-men were at first completely unregulated, and there was no limit on the number of slaves they could carry. It was of no benefit to a shipmaster to have slaves die on the voyage through overcrowding in the hold, but it is fair to say that cattle in transport often fared better than the slaves. Thanks to the efforts of the early anti-slavery campaigners, an Act was passed by the British Parliament in 1788 which limited the number of slaves carried to five males per 3 tons burthen. As might be expected, with little or no attempt being made to inspect ships, the Act was largely ignored by the slavers.

In Britain, the ports of London, Bristol, Liverpool and Glasgow were all heavily involved in the slave trade, but by the end of the 18th century Liverpool had become the main focus, its ships handling 90 per cent of the combined trade of Britain and Europe. There was a good reason for the port's dominance – Liverpool being within easy reach of the manufacturing towns of the Midlands, which produced most of the goods required to exchange for slaves in Africa. In a few short years Liverpool grew from an obscure village on the banks of the Mersey to the busiest port in Europe. Liverpudlians, from the lowliest clerk to the richest speculator, were almost all, in one way or another, involved in this booming trade that provided employment for so many and made fortunes overnight for those with money to invest.

At the height of the transatlantic slave trade it is estimated that 130,000 British seamen made their living from it, while countless thousands ashore were employed in servicing and supplying their ships. In the factories of the industrial Midlands armies of workers were involved in producing goods to barter for slaves. Britain's major ports and cities grew fat on the exploitation of Africa's poor. To be fair to many of those ashore involved in this vile trade, they were, by and large, blissfully ignorant of the terrible suffering they were a party to.

Ideally, the owners of the slavers aimed to operate their vessels on a triangular trade, carrying cloth, cheap jewellery, pots and pans, guns, powder and alcohol to West Africa, where these were bartered for slaves, who were then transported to the colonies across the Atlantic. Having discharged and sold their live cargoes, the ships then returned home with sugar, cotton, tobacco and other produce from the plantations to which they were supplying the labour. As Samuel Plimsoll had not yet appeared on the scene, there were few rules governing the safe operation of commercial shipping. For the would-be entrepreneurs this was a dream and they queued up to invest their money. Any rotting old hulk capable of being patched up was pressed into service and sent to sea. With an average net profit of £40,000 (nearly £2 million in today's money) being made on a round voyage, investors had nothing to lose and everything to gain. The master of a slaver would earn around £5 a month in wages, but with a bonus of up to 3 per cent payable on slaves delivered alive, his due reward would often be over £1000 for a voyage, no mean sum in those days. Ship's officers and petty officers were often able to supplement their wages by carrying a few slaves of their own for sale.

At the time, Britain was frequently at war with both France and Spain, and some slavers who carried letters of marque supplemented their income with a little legalised piracy. A letter of marque, issued to a British ship by the Lord High Admiral, licensed the commander of a privately owned ship to cruise in search of and to seize enemy merchant vessels.

The Liverpool three-master *Enterprize*, owned by Thomas Leyland and commanded by Captain Cesar Lawson, sailed from Liverpool in July 1803 bearing a letter of marque, bound for the Bonny River. Manned by a crew of sixty-five, she had on board a cargo of cotton goods, gunpowder, muskets, wine, brandy, ironmongery, earthenware, umbrellas and cheap trinkets, worth in all around £9000. Lawson's orders were to barter his cargo in exchange for slaves, ivory and palm oil and, of course, to engage in privateering whenever the opportunity presented itself. Instructions given to Captain Lawson regarding the latter were precise: 'We have taken out letters of marque against the French and Batavian republic, and if you are fortunate enough to fall in with and capture any of their vessels, send the same to this port, under the care of an active prize master, and a sufficient number of men out of your ship; and also put a copy of commission on board her, but do not molest any neutral ship, as it would involve us in expensive lawsuits and subject us to heavy damages... .' To assist her in her privateering, the *Enterprize* mounted a formidable array of guns and carronades.

Thomas Leyland's investment in guns soon paid dividends. On the passage south Lawson fell in with the Spanish brig *St Augustin*, boarded her, and sent her back to Liverpool with a prize crew. Later in the voyage he boarded and recaptured the Liverpool ship *John*, taken as a prize by the French. The *John* had 261 slaves on board, whom Lawson sent to Dominica to be sold.

The *Enterprize* reached Bonny on 23 September, where her cargo was quickly traded for 412 slaves. Having loaded a quantity of ivory, hardwoods and sugar in addition to the slaves, she then set out on her 5,500-mile Atlantic crossing. Favourable winds made for a fast passage, and Lawson arrived in Havana with 392 slaves still alive and in 'good condition.' After settling all dues, the *Enterprize*'s owners made a net profit on the round voyage, Liverpool to Liverpool, of £24,430.

As would be expected, the only ones not to benefit from this profitable business were the unfortunate slaves themselves. Even in an age when poverty and deprivation were the daily lot of the peasantry of Europe, conditions prevailing on board the slavers were beyond belief. Some captains – more with an eye to greater profit than the welfare of their human cargo – limited the number of slaves they took on board in the hope that more would arrive at their destination alive and reasonably fit; but this was far from being the norm. The more common practice was to cram as many slaves into the hold as space would allow, paying no regard to human dignity, physical wellbeing or sanitation. Naked and manacled two by two, they were laid side by side on bare boards at the bottom of the hold, packed so tightly that they closely resembled sardines in a tin. Often a second deck was built and another layer of slaves laid on it, so that the headroom for each layer was reduced to a mere 30 inches or so.

Today animal rights protestors wax incandescent over the conditions in which live animals are transported by road. Would that the African slaves had travelled in such comfort. Furthermore, whereas animals on their way to market, even when crossing to the Continent and driving deep into Europe, are rarely cooped up in their trucks for more than a day or two, the slaves faced a long and uncomfortable ocean voyage. Whether taking the comparatively short 2,700-mile route to Brazil, or the so-called 'Middle Passage' to the West Indies – more than twice that distance – the ships, all under sail, were at the mercy of wind and current, often being more than three months at sea. In such crowded conditions, having little food or water, and usually lying in their own excrement, the slaves easily fell prey to the killer diseases smallpox, yellow fever, cholera and dysentery. Many went blind with opthalmia, others went mad or, overcome by the sheer hopelessness of their predicament, simply willed themselves to die – and die they did. It was accepted that around 15 per cent of a slaver's cargo would, in one way or another, not live to see the land.

There is no shortage of written evidence as to conditions in slavers. Dr Alexander Falconbridge, in An Account of the Slave Trade on the Coast of Africa, published in London in 1788, wrote:

> ...they are frequently stowed so close as to admit no other posture than lying on their side. Neither will the height between decks, unless directly under the grating, permit them the indulgence of an erect posture...The hardships and inconveniences suffered by the Negroes during the passage are scarcely to be enumerated or conceived. They are far more violently affected by the seasickness than the Europeans. It frequently terminates in death, especially amongst the women. But the exclusion of fresh air is among the most intolerable. For the purpose of admitting this needful refreshment, most of the ships in the slave trade are provided, between decks, with five or six air-ports on each side of the ship, of about six inches in length and four in breadth, in addition to which, some few ships, but not one in twenty, have what they denominate wind-sails. But whenever the sea is rough and the rain heavy, it becomes necessary to shut these, and every other conveyance by which air is admitted. The fresh air being thus excluded, the Negroes' rooms very soon grow intolerably hot. The confined air, rendered noxious by the effluvia exhaled from their bodies, and by being repeatedly breathed, soon produces fevers and fluxes, which generally carries off great numbers of them...

The seaman of the 18th century had never given too much thought to hold ventilation, being more concerned with keeping his ship watertight. When the cargo consisted of inanimate bales and boxes, apart from possible sweat damage little harm was done when the holds were battened down in heavy weather. But when several hundred living slaves were confined in total darkness in an airless hold then the effect was inevitably catastrophic.

Commodore Charles Bullen, commanding HMS *Brazen*, after boarding a Brazilian brig of 212 tons with 525 slaves on board in the Gulf of Guinea, reported to the Admiralty:

> I have to assure your Lordships that the extent of human misery encountered, as evinced by these unfortunate beings, is almost impossible for me to describe. They were all confined in a most crowded state below, and many in irons, which latter were released as soon as they could be got at. The putrid atmosphere emitting from the slave deck was horrible in the extreme, and so inhuman are these fellow creature dealers that several of those confined at the farther end of the slave room were obliged to be dragged on deck in an almost lifeless state, and wasted away to mere shadows, never having breathed fresh air since their embarkation. Many females had infants at their breasts, and all were crowded together in a solid mass of filth and corruption, several suffering from dysentery, and although but a fortnight on board, sixty-seven of them had died from that complaint.

Slaves in transit at sea may have suffered the torments of Hell itself but, if anything, the seamen who manned the ships often fared worse. Not only did they have to endure the fearful dangers involved in scouring the rivers and creeks of West Africa in search of slaves, but being of less commercial value than the cargo they carried, they were often treated accordingly. The pay was poor, the food worse, and tyrannical captains inflicted the harshest punishment for the slightest misdemeanour. Of this, Olaudah Equiano, a literate slave carried in a British ship in 1788, wrote: 'I had never seen among my people such instances of brutal cruelty; and this not only shewn towards us blacks, but also to some of the whites themselves. One white man in particular I saw, when we were permitted to be on deck, flogged so unmercifully with a large rope near the foremast that he died in consequence of it; and they tossed him over the side as they would have done a brute.'

It was accepted that on average some 20 per cent of a slaver's crew would die on the voyage, whether from disease, murder by mutinous slaves, by flogging on board, or just from sheer exhaustion. In addition, another 20 per cent were permanently crippled. Others, so sickened by their treatment on the voyage, deserted on reaching the far side of the Atlantic, which then conveniently relieved the master and owners of the obligation to pay them any wages due. Cynics might say that the treatment meted out to these men was designed to that end.

In the early days, when the transatlantic slave trade was first beginning to be seen as a profitable enterprise, the method of collecting slaves was uncomplicated. It was then a simple matter of anchoring offshore and contacting the caboceers, an unsavoury bunch of half-castes who acted as middlemen between the whites and the local chiefs. The slaves, previously rounded up in dawn raids on the villages, were then brought out to the ships in canoes. Some of the more determined captains took their ships far inland, skillfully navigating the creeks, then sending their boats into the jungle; but innocent though the natives were, they soon learned it was wise to disappear into the bush as soon as a ship was sighted. However, there were great dangers to be faced by the bold slave hunter, as illustrated by a letter written by Henry Harrison in April 1759:

On the 12th of January, we had the misfortune to be cut off by the negroes; they killed Captain Potter, our surgeon, carpenter, cooper, and James Steward, a boy. Luckily, the captain had sent me on shore that morning to go to the King's town, about 10 miles up the river, to fetch the slaves down; but before I reached the town, I met two of his servants bringing a slave down; returned with them; made a smoke on shore as a signal for our boat, but before I had well made it, saw her put off from the vessel with six of our people in her, being all left alive on board. I swam off to her and we rowed for the *Spencer*, Captain Daniel Cooke, then lying at Cape Mount.

At one o'clock that night, Captain Cooke got under way,

27

and made sail in order to attempt to recover our vessel; at daylight, finding her at anchor, he fired his guns into her for about an hour, but I could not persuade him to board her. That evening the slaves ran the snow on shore. We had purchased 103 slaves, and had a pledge for two more on board. The slaves and natives would not give us the least article of wearing apparel.

When this fatal accident happened, our chief mate was gone with the yawl to windward, and the boatswain with the long boat to leeward to purchase slaves. Mr. Eaton and the boatswain got on board Captain Nichols, and I heard that they saved 15 or 16 slaves that were due to us on shore, and left Mana, Mar. 30, destined for the West Indies. I am now moved to the brig *Industry*, Captain Banks, and we intend to sail for Antigua tomorrow, having 122 slaves, all in good health, on board. They have buried Richard Worthington and three more of their people.

It is all too easily accepted in today's climate of political correctness that the white man was solely responsible for the enslavement of Africans on a large scale in the 18th and 19th centuries. The truth is somewhat at odds with this theory. It may be that the white man's insatiable quest for labour to cultivate the fields of his colonial empires created the demand, and it cannot be denied that he, and he alone, provided the means of transport; but it was the unsuppressed brutality and greed of other Africans, and in particular their rulers, that satisfied this demand. The local chiefs – or kings, as they preferred to be called – held absolute power over their subjects, and had no compunction in selling them into slavery in exchange for the cheap trash, the guns and alcohol that the white man offered. Any minor crime, even the theft of a scrap of clothing, was sufficient grounds for a man to be seized and sold to the dealers, often for as little as a watered-down bottle of rum. And when this alone was not enough to meet the increasing demand, the chiefs resorted to more direct methods. The self-styled 'King of Barsally', who held sway over much of the River Gambia, had a novel approach to the problem, as described by Francis Moore, a trader on the river. 'It is to that insatiable thirst of his after brandy that his subjects' freedoms and families are in so precarious a situation: for being intoxicated he very often goes with some of his troops by a town in the daytime, and returns in the night, and sets fire to three parts of it, and sets guards to the fourth to seize the people as they run out from the fire; he ties their arms behind them, and marches them to the place where he sells them...' But by far the most infamous of West African monarchs was King Tegbesu of Dahomey, who towards the end of the 18th century was said to be selling more than 9000 slaves a year, mainly to the Spanish and Portuguese. Tegbesu's annual income was estimated as around £250,000, a vast sum for the day, and far in excess of that earned by any white slaver.

Internal wars provided another major source of slaves. Before extensive colonisation by the Europeans, most of Africa was in a constant state of war, with tribe fighting tribe and village fighting village – a state to which this great continent is now, sadly, returning. The survivors on the losing side of a battle were invariably taken as slaves by their conquerors, and when the demand came, sold on to the white traders. Increased demand created more wars, and so more prisoners were taken and more innocents enslaved. It has been said of the white slave trader that his guilt lay not so much in the buying of slaves, as in providing the incentive for Africans to make perpetual war on each other.

When, and this was quite often the case, the chiefs ran out of locally acquired slaves, they turned to their Arab brothers in the north to make up the deficit. As a result, for the unfortunate slaves the ordeal was cruelly prolonged. Rounded up like cattle, and herded into centrally placed 'slave markets', they were held in pens until their numbers were sufficient to make up a caravan, or 'coffle', for the march to the coast. Then, shackled together, and carrying heavy loads of provisions and ivory on their heads, the slaves, men, women and children, were forced to trek often up to 1000 miles through hostile territory to the coast. They were given little rest, food was minimal, and the whip was used unsparingly on those who failed to keep up. The only escape was through death, and this was the fate of many. Their bones marked a trail of misery through desert and jungle to the slaving ports, where the survivors were ushered into another living hell. A vivid description of the treatment of slaves when they reached the coast was given by John Bardot, an agent for the French Royal African Company:

As the slaves come down from the inland country, they are put into a booth, or prison, built for that purpose near the beach, all of them together; and when the Europeans are to receive them, every part of every one of them, to the smallest member, men and women being all stark naked. Such as are allowed good and sound, are set on one side, and the others by themselves; which slaves so rejected are there called Mackrons, being above thirty-five years of age, or defective in their limbs, eyes or teeth, or grown grey, or that have the venereal disease, or any other imperfection. These being set aside, each of the others, which have passed as good, is marked on the breast with a red hot iron...

The branded slaves, after this, are returned to their former booth, where the factor is to subsist them at his own charge, which amounts to about two-pence a day for each of them, with bread and water, which is all their allowance. There continues sometimes ten or fifteen days, till the sea is still enough to send them aboard...Before they enter the canoes, or come out of the booth, their former Black masters strip them of every rag they have, without distinction of men or women; to supply which, in orderly ships, each of them as they come aboard is allowed a piece of canvas to wrap around their waist, which is very acceptable to these poor wretches...

On occasions, rare perhaps, conditions on board ship for the slaves became so intolerable that they resorted to mutiny. As the crews of the slavers were always heavily armed, these desperate rebellions were usually short-lived, often ending in bloody retribution. However, there was one notable exception.

The Spanish-owned brig *Amistad*, commanded by Captain Ramon Ferrer, was on a coastal passage between ports in Cuba carrying fifty-three slaves when she ran into adverse winds. What should have been a few days at sea ran into weeks. Food was short, and a rumour circulated amongst the slaves, who were not long out of Africa, that the white men were planning to kill and eat them. One of their number, Sengbeh Pieh, said to be the son of a Mende chief, organised a mutiny. In the dead of night the slaves broke free of their irons, armed themselves with machetes which they found in the hold, and swarmed on deck. In the melee

30

that followed Captain Ferrer and the cook were killed, and the rest of the crew escaped in a small boat.

Also on board the *Amistad* were the two Spaniards who owned the slaves. These men were spared on condition that they sailed the ship to Africa. The slaves being totally ignorant of navigation, the Spaniards sailed north, and the *Amistad* ended up in American waters off Long Island. The ship was boarded by the Coast Guard, and towed into port. Sengbeh and his collaborators were put on trial, charged with mutiny on the high seas and murder, but with the help of a group of abolitionists were freed.

The vast majority of slaver captains were cruel or just indifferent to the plight of the slaves they carried, and almost without exception losses on the ocean passage were heavy, on average 15 per cent not living to see the other side. There were some humanitarians on the poop, however. One such was Captain Hugh Crow, who commanded ships on the transatlantic slave trade for eighteen years. By all accounts Crow was a brave commander, having successfully fought a number of battles with French privateers, but he was also a kind and conscientious man. He was noted for his concern for the welfare of his crews and, more unusually, of the slaves he carried, issuing lime juice to both to prevent scurvy, and in the case of the slaves ensuring that they were well fed and their quarters regularly cleaned out. His attention to the welfare of those in his care paid dividends, and he rarely lost a man, above or below decks, on the long ocean passages. Whenever he brought a ship into Kingston, Jamaica, the word went around, 'Crow has come again, and as usual his whites and blacks are as plump as cotton bags.'

There were shipowners who cared, too, albeit with an ulterior motive. Humphrey Morice, a London merchant, Member of Parliament and sometime Governor of the Bank of England, ran a fleet of eight ships in the trade. Being a person of some standing in the City, he maintained a respectable image by sending his ships out from London loaded with general cargo for Rotterdam. But after discharging in the Dutch port they surreptitiously filled their holds with gunpowder, spirits, cloth, pots and pans, and all the other goods in great demand by the European traders on the coast, and sailed for West Africa.

In the Slave Rivers, Morice's captains exchanged their cargoes

31

for gold, with which they then bought slaves, later selling them on to Portuguese traders, who were always in the market for good blacks. In this way Morice avoided the heavy losses his ships would probably have incurred if they carried the slaves to the West Indies or America. On the rare occasions when it was impossible to sell the slaves on the coast, Morice had no option but to send them across the Atlantic. Then, always with an eye to business, Morice put a doctor aboard the ship and instructed the captain to buy limes to combat an outbreak of scurvy. Sufficient food, regular exercise, and attention paid to the health of the slaves ensured that Morice's losses on passage were markedly less than those of others in the trade.

In his lifetime, Humphrey Morice made a substantial fortune out of slave trading, but despite his shrewd business sense he was heavily in debt when he died. Most of his fortune, it was later revealed, went on large donations to the Whig Party, which he hoped would secure him a seat in the House of Lords. Unlike many of the donors to political parties of today, he was disappointed, and died plain Mister Morice.

The main embarkation ports for slaves in the Gulf of Guinea lay in the two bights, the Bight of Benin and the Bight of Biafra. It was in the latter bight, into which flowed the rivers forming the great Niger Delta, that the British did most of their slave gathering. Here was Africa at its darkest, the notorious Slave Rivers, the Benin, Escravos, Forcados, Nun, Brass, Sambreiro, Bonny, Opobo, Kwa Ibo and Calabar, an evil place steeped in witchcraft and cannibalism. At the heart of this sink of iniquity was the last mentioned Calabar River, down which a quarter of all the slaves carried across the Atlantic passed. Sluggish, often shrouded in a thick, low mist, the Calabar winds its way to the sea through dense mangrove forests, past such sinister milestones as Tom Shot Point, Alligator Island, Escape Channel, and Smoke Flats. The slave coffles were brought to Calabar Town, 40 miles inland, where the terrified captives were then bundled into canoes and paddled down river to ships anchored off the bar. Two centuries later, although oil in vast quantities has been discovered in the area, the Calabar River is still haunted by the ghosts of the thousands of black slaves it once transported into permanent exile. An air of sadness lies over the river, due in part, perhaps, to

32

the fact that the people who live on its banks are still as poor and ignorant as their enslaved ancestors. The oil wealth which should have brought them prosperity and happiness has been squandered by a succession of corrupt governments.

Chapter Four

Pirates and Reformers

Amazing grace! How sweet the sound
That saved a wretch like me!
I was once lost, but now am found,
Was blind, but now I see.

Captain John Newton

Some 3000 miles to the north of the Calabar River, in the Welsh county of Pembrokeshire, lies the tiny hamlet of Little Newcastle, a collection of half a dozen stone-built cottages, a pub and a church. Here, in 1682, was born Bartholomew Roberts, the most successful sea pirate of all time.

Barti Roberts went to sea in merchant ships at an early age and, as was inevitable at the time, he soon became involved in the slave trade. In the summer of 1719 he was sailing as third mate in the London slaver *Princess* in the Gulf of Guinea when she was attacked by pirates led by a fellow Welshman, the notorious Howell Davis, in the *Royal Rover*. The *Princess* was forced to strike her colours, and Roberts was captured. Perhaps because of his Celtic origins, but more likely for his ability to navigate, Roberts' life was spared, but only on condition that he signed on with Davis in the *Royal Rover*.

Competent navigators were at a premium on the pirate circuit, and it was not long before Roberts was sharing the poop with Howell Davis; six weeks after his capture, he found himself in command of the *Royal Rover*. Davis had been killed in a Portuguese ambush on Principe Island, and having extricated themselves from a very nasty situation, the *Royal Rover*'s crew spread all sail and escaped out to sea. On that same day they elected Bartholomew Roberts as their captain. They chose wisely. While the tea-drinking, teetotaller Roberts turned out to be a strict disciplinarian, who would allow no alcohol, gambling or women aboard his ship, his skill as a buccaneer proved to be second to none. Roberts began his new career by sailing the *Royal Rover* to the Caribbean, and over the two years that followed seized more than 400 ships, reaping for himself and his crew a fortune in excess of £80 million.

Early in 1721, with all shipping in the Caribbean at a standstill as a result of his piratical activities, Roberts returned to the Gulf of Guinea, where the flourishing slave trade was attracting ships of all nationalities. There, with a newly acquired ship aptly named *Royal Fortune*, he opened his campaign by sailing boldly into Sierra Leone harbour with the skull and crossbones flying. With typical abandon he bombarded the British fort into submission, and then boarded, pillaged, and set fire to six slavers anchored in the river. Bartholomew Roberts, or 'Black Bart', as he was now known, had arrived on the West Coast.

Continuing on south, Roberts fell in with the Royal Africa Company's frigate *Onslow*, which he captured intact. As the *Onslow* was a superior ship to his own, Roberts transferred his flag to her, increased her armament to forty guns, and renamed her *Royal Fortune* for his old ship. He was no doubt confident that his career on this side of the Atlantic would soon prosper, as it had done in American waters.

By now, word had reached London that Bartholomew Roberts was in the Gulf of Guinea, and two 60-gun frigates, HMS *Swallow*, commanded by Captain Chaloner Ogle, and HMS *Weymouth*, with Captain Mungo Herdman in command, were dispatched from Spithead. Ogle was the senior commander, sailing with orders that were brief and specific – to put a stop to Black Bart's nefarious activities without delay.

While the frigates were on passage, Roberts moved into the Bight of Biafra, sacking and plundering as he went, and creating havoc amongst shipping on the coast, as he had so recently done in the Caribbean. In November he put into the Calabar River with two other newly acquired ships, the *Great Ranger* and *Little Ranger*, in support.

As yet unaware that the Royal Navy was searching for him,

Roberts decided to take advantage of the seclusion of the Calabar River to careen his ships, while at the same time attempting to trade with the local chiefs. Work on the ships progressed well, but the pirates' unscrupulous methods of trading resulted in a series of fierce and prolonged pitched battles with the locals. To this day Bartholomew Roberts and his men are still remembered in the stories told around the cooking fires of the villages on the banks of the Calabar River.

When news finally reached Roberts that the Navy was in pursuit it was late December, and tired of the continuing battles with the locals, he said farewell to Calabar and sailed south for Cape Lopez, casting around for likely prizes as he went.

It so happened that at the time there was a dearth of shipping in the southern waters of the Bight, and Roberts made no more captures on the way. Arriving off Cape Lopez, he spent a few days searching the rivers and creeks of the coast of Gabon for victims then, still having no success, headed back to the north. He assumed that by this time his pursuers must have given up the chase and returned to their base at Sierra Leone. Had he called in at Principe Island on the way north, he would have learned to the contrary. The two Navy frigates, *Swallow* and *Weymouth*, were in fact anchored in the lee of the island, and had been there for some time. Captain Ogle had decided to put in to Principe for provisions and water, intending to stay no more than a few days, but while they were anchored off, malaria swept through the two ships. One hundred men had died, and many others were still sick. When at last Ogle was able to muster sufficient fit men to man his ships, he set sail for the Gold Coast, where at Cape Coast Castle, a port frequented by many British merchant ships trading to West Africa, he hoped to be able to press-gang enough men to take him on to Sierra Leone.

While Ogle kicked his heels and fumed, Black Bart's little fleet had sailed past Cape Coast Castle undetected. Roberts moved west to Cape Palmas, but he found the seas there just as empty of shipping as they were off Cape Lopez. In desperation, he then decided to return east to Whydah, hugging the coast as he went. Whydah, 240 miles east of Cape Coast Castle, and close to Lagos, was then the busiest slaving post on the coast, and Roberts was confident that here he would find rich pickings. His confidence was vindicated, for when the three heavily armed pirate ships were sighted, every one of the slavers anchored off Whydah surrendered without a shot being fired. All except one were then ransomed for a payment to Roberts of eight pounds of gold dust (about £500) each, thus adding to the pirate's growing hoard. The one exception, whose captain refused to pay the ransom, was set on fire, and the eighty unfortunate slaves on board, who were still in irons, either perished in the fire or jumped overboard. Some drowned, the rest were torn to pieces by the waiting sharks.

Unknown to Black Bart, his ships had been sighted when passing Cape Coast Castle eastbound, and Chaloner Ogle's frigates, now fully manned, were soon under full sail for Whydah. When news reached the Welshman of the Royal Navy's approach, he lost no time in heading south again. When Ogle arrived in Whydah, the King of Whydah, incensed by Roberts' audacity, offered him the vast sum of fifty-six pounds of gold dust for the capture of the pirate.

It is not known whether Captain Ogle returned to Whydah to collect his reward, but he certainly put an end to the activities of Bartholomew Roberts. Running ahead of *Weymouth* in *Swallow*, Ogle caught up with the pirate fleet off Cape Lopez on 5 February 1722. The *Royal Fortune* and her two consorts were anchored close in to the cape, and mistook the approaching frigate for a merchant ship. Roberts sent the *Great Ranger* out to take what appeared to be an easy prize, only to see her go down under the *Swallow*'s powerful guns. As the *Great Ranger*, afire from stem to stern, slowly disappeared beneath the waves, HMS *Weymouth* appeared on the horizon, and Roberts, not wishing to take on a superior force, weighed anchor and fled.

Five days later, Ogle overhauled the *Royal Fortune*, and in the fierce battle that followed, Bartholomew Roberts was killed on the poop of his ship. He died still hurling defiance at his enemy, but with his death the fight went out of his crew, and they eventually struck their colours to the *Swallow*. Those who survived, fifty-two in all, were taken back to Cape Coast Castle in irons, and there, on 20 April 1722, they were hanged on the beach.

So ended the career of the infamous Bartholomew Roberts, who in the last months of his life – quite unintentionally, it must be said, played a part in the suppression of the African slave trade, even if it was only by taking out of circulation many of the ships and men involved. Others, men of higher integrity and with different motives, would follow in his wake, for in Europe, and more particularly in Britain, attitudes to slavery were changing.

On 24 July 1725 John Newton was born in London, son of the captain of a merchant ship sailing regularly to the Mediterranean. As was the common practice of the day, young Newton went to sea in his father's ship at a very early age, learning the profession from the keel up. He remained in merchant ships until in 1744, aged nineteen, he was unfortunate enough to walk into the arms of the press gang while on shore. Shortly afterwards he found himself aboard the man-of-war HMS *Harwich*, where his seafaring experience was immediately recognised, and he was promoted to midshipman. Although he was a junior officer sailing in the half-deck, Newton found conditions on board the naval ship intolerable, and he deserted at the earliest opportunity. Unfortunately, before he was able to disappear inland, he was picked up and returned to his ship, where he was publicly flogged and then demoted to ordinary seaman.

In the course of time John Newton was released from the King's Service, and found a berth in a slaver, eventually rising to command. This was hardly the pinnacle of a seagoing career that he had hoped to achieve, but he was in good company, and the rewards were commensurate with the demands of the calling. Older now, Newton had developed strong religious convictions. It was his custom to assemble his crew twice a day for prayers, yet, at the same time, the treatment he meted out to the slaves he carried was as harsh as that of any slaver captain. But then, this was an age of contradictions.

Newton's conversion to religion stemmed – or so he claimed – from an experience he had when his ship was near to foundering in a violent storm. In desperation, he went down on his knees and called on God – or any god willing to listen – to save the ship. The storm promptly subsided, and John Newton thereafter became an enthusiastic Christian, composing in gratitude for his deliverance a hymn so hauntingly beautiful that it still enjoys immense popularity today. The first verse tells the story:

> *Amazing grace! How sweet the sound*
> *That saved a wretch like me!*

I was once lost, but now am found,
Was blind, but now I see.

The origin of the melody is lost in the mists of time, but it is
believed that Newton might have taken it from a tune his slaves
hummed in the abject misery of their transportation.

The watches are long at sea, and in the idle hours John Newton
made good use of his books, acquiring, amongst other things, a
fair knowledge of Latin. But his first love was the sea, and he
would have continued sailing, had he not been struck down by
illness, and in 1755 was forced to find employment ashore. For
five years he was Surveyor of Tides at Liverpool, but in 1760 he
finally found his true calling, being ordained a clergyman. He was
appointed curate of the parish of Olney in Buckinghamshire,
where he spent twenty happy years, and became a prolific writer
of hymns. In 1780 he moved to St. Mary Woolnoth in the City of
London as rector, and was soon drawing huge congregations with
his powerful sermons, many of which were on the abolition of the
slave trade. One who listened earnestly to Newton's preaching
was William Wilberforce.

William Wilberforce was the very antithesis of John Newton.
Born in Hull in 1759 of wealthy parents, he had led a sheltered
and privileged life, going first to boarding school, then to
Cambridge. Like many well-placed young men of the day, his
ambition was to go into politics, and he was elected Member of
Parliament for Hull at the age of 21. An educated man and a
brilliant public speaker, his career in politics was assured, and he
might well have lived a very comfortable, if scarcely useful, life
had he not met John Newton.

Wilberforce was a regular attender at St. Mary Woolnoth, and
in time he began to warm towards the Reverend Captain
Newton's message. Newton eventually convinced Wilberforce of
the iniquity of the slave trade and persuaded him to use his
influence in Parliament to bring about its end. He also introduced
him to two other anti-slavery campaigners, Granville Sharp and
Thomas Clarkson. Sharp, later to be accepted as the real father of
the abolition movement, was born in 1735, the son of a
Northumberland clergyman. As a boy, he was apprenticed to a
local linen draper for seven years, but as soon as he was released

from his indentures, he moved to London, where he earned a living as clerk in the Ordnance Department. His detestation of slavery began when he found a Negro slave lying in a London gutter after being severely beaten by his master. The encounter led him to a study of the law in relation to slavery, and eventual participation in the abolition movement. Thomas Clarkson, also the son of a clergyman, was, like Wilberforce, a Cambridge graduate converted to the fight against slavery. A great deal of his time was spent visiting slave ships at ports around the country, talking to their crews and observing the conditions in which slaves were carried. The knowledge gained he used to write a series of powerful essays and pamphlets condemning the trade and urging its abolition.

In 1787 the three men, with the support of the Quaker movement, formed the Society for the Abolition of the Slave Trade. They were an unlikely trio to be fighting for the rights of the underdog, but their talents were eminently suited to the task they had undertaken. Wilberforce was a brilliant parliamentary speaker and a close friend of Prime Minister William Pitt, Sharp was a grandson of the Archbishop of York and employed in the Tower of London, while Clarkson was a skilful propagandist.

The time was right for change, there being many in Britain who had begun to question not just the morality of slavery but the need for it at all. Steam power had arrived and very soon the world economy would no longer need to rely heavily on manual labour, free or otherwise.

There was no better place for the campaigners to start their work than in their own country, for Britain had at least 15,000 African slaves, most of them domestic servants brought back from the West Indies by retiring colonists. In 1772 Granville Sharp set the ball rolling by bringing to court the case of a black slave, James Somerset. Under English law, no man had the right to enslave another, although the validity of this law was somewhat obscure when applied to black immigrants. Somerset had escaped from his master, was recaptured, and on the point of being shipped back to the West Indies in irons, when Sharp took up his case. The court battle was long and hard, for there were powerful vested interests involved. In the end, the case came before Lord Chief Justice Mansfield, who was forced to adjudicate in James Somerset's favour. Mansfield's ruling, somewhat reluctantly arrived at, was that 'the state of slavery is so odious that nothing can be suffered to support it but positive law, and there is no law.' He ordered Somerset to be discharged a free man. From that day on, 22 June 1722, all slaves in Britain were recognised as free men and women.

The ruling was just, and long overdue, but the problem then arose as to what could be done with 15,000 poor Africans who were literally thrown out on the streets overnight. Some found jobs, but the vast majority of the freed slaves, who had led sheltered lives in their captivity, were unable to fend for themselves. Many took to stealing and begging, becoming a nuisance to the indigenous population.

Granville Sharp had a plan to deal with the problem. His proposal, so simple that it bordered on the naïve, was to send all the slaves back to Africa, whence they had originally come. He consulted a Swedish botanist, Dr Henry Smeathan, an acknowledged expert on Africa, who suggested that a new home be found for the freed slaves in Sierra Leone. Here, Smeathan said, they would enjoy an 'extraordinary temperature and salubrity of climate.' The Government, no doubt anxious to solve what was threatening to be a major problem, offered financial help towards the transport to West Africa, and in 1786 the 'Sierra Leone Plan' was born. With backing from his Quaker friends Sharp chartered two ships, the *Belisarius* and the *Atlantic*.

At first, the repatriation was voluntary but, by the end of November 1786, of the 600 or more expected only 105 were on board the *Belisarius*, and 154 on the *Atlantic*, both of which were lying at Gravesend. December came, and no more potential settlers came forward for Sierra Leone. In desperation, the Vagrancy Act was invoked, warning that any blacks found begging or loitering in the streets would be forcibly put on board the ships. This had little effect on the freed slaves, who had become accustomed to a comfortable life in Britain. They had no wish to be transported to this so-called African Utopia, and simply melted into the underworld of the big cities.

In January 1787 the ships still lay in Gravesend and there was unrest on board. The 259 voluntary emigrants, men, women and children, had been incarcerated on board for many weeks, their food was running short, and morale was at rock bottom. To aggravate further an already inflammatory situation, the weather then turned bitterly cold. A daily ration of rum, presumably issued to ease matters, only resulted in a great deal of drunkenness in the ships and more unrest.

Something had to be done, and quickly. By now, the *Belisarius* had 184 passengers on board, and the *Atlantic* 242, and orders were given to sail the ships from Gravesend on 16 January. *The Times* newspaper reported: 'The two ships having on board as many of those people as could be collected sailed from Gravesend on Thursday last, with a fair wind, for Sierra Leone, on the coast of Africa, where they are to be landed, in order to form the intended new settlement.'

The Times's report was over optimistic, as none of the equipment needed for the colony, tents, agricultural tools, weapons and gunpowder, had yet been loaded. The 'fair wind' carried *Belisarius* and *Atlantic* only as far as Plymouth Sound. And while they lay at anchor there the situation went from bad to worse. Some of the settlers went ashore in search of food and warm clothing, and their presence on the streets greatly disturbed the citizens of Plymouth. The local authorities began to fear they might be faced with an invasion of poor blacks, and prevailed upon the Admiralty to curtail shore leave from the ships.

While the two ships lay in Plymouth, they were joined by a third, the *Vernon*, bringing the number of settlers for Sierra Leone to 643, among them sixty white women. These women claimed that they had been plied with drink, and when they were incapable, married to black men without their consent. The official version was that they were 'women of the lowest sort, in ill health and of bad character,' and their abduction – for that is what it was – seems to have been part of a plan to clear the streets of London of undesirables, and at the same time provided breeding females for the new colony.

The three ships were still nowhere near full, but all attempts to round up more volunteers for the expedition failed. Winter turned to spring and, following an outbreak of fever on board, Captain Thomas Thompson, who was in overall command, was ordered to take the ships to sea. Before they sailed, the ex-slaves and their women were joined by thirteen white men, skilled artisans, who it was hoped would be able to organise the building of suitable housing in Sierra Leone. Escorted by the sloop HMS *Nautilus*, the *Belisarius, Atlantic* and *Vernon*, all by now heavily barnacled and the worse for wear after their long stay in port, their crews and passengers in a mutinous mood, finally left Plymouth Sound on 8 April. The voyage ahead promised to be a difficult one.

The winds were fair, and the ships reached the Canary Islands on the 21st, anchoring off Tenerife, where they were to take on stores and water. Captain Thompson reported back to the Admiralty: 'I have the satisfaction to acquaint you that I arrived here yesterday at noon, with the three transports after a very quick passage of thirteen days from Plymouth, and that the blacks have hitherto conducted themselves remarkably well, but I am sorry to say that fourteen have died since our departure from England.' A further seventy were to die before Sierra Leone was reached – and that was only the beginning of the settlers' troubles.

Granville Sharp and the Committee for the Black Poor, advised by Dr Smeathan, firmly believed they were sending the settlers out to a land flowing with milk and honey, where they would quickly establish themselves and prosper. Reality proved otherwise. When the fleet anchored in the Sierra Leone river in June, Thompson went ashore to negotiate a land settlement with the local chiefs. He met with King Tom and others who, for trade goods worth £59, sold him a 200 square-mile parcel of land which Thompson described as, 'a fine tract of mountainous country covered with trees of all kinds.' Tents were set up and plots marked out for the building of houses, and the new settlement was named Granville Town after the man who had inspired the expedition. Unfortunately, the settlers had arrived in the middle of the rainy season – the worst rainy season seen for many years.

Sierra Leone, situated 8 degrees north of the Equator, derives its name from the mountains that ridge this lush peninsula of land. When the Portuguese navigator Pedro de Sintra landed there in 1462, it was during the six month-long rainy season, and the continuous roar of thunder that reverberated around the hills led him to call his discovery Serra Leôa (Lion Mountains). This was later corrupted to Sierra Leone. Over the years the territory earned the reputation as the 'white man's grave', and not without good cause. The torrential rains, averaging 32 inches a month in the

43

long rainy season, produce a very unhealthy climate. Malaria, dysentery, beriberi, smallpox, conjunctivitis, rheumatism, elephantiasis and several nasty skin diseases are endemic. And not surprisingly, the twin spectres of apathy and alcoholism are always present.

For the first six months, while the food brought by the ships lasted, the blacks and their white advisors made an effort to establish themselves in the new land, but the incessant rain, disease and drunkenness all took their toll. When the rains finally stopped, and it was found that nothing they planted in the sodden soil would grow, most of them lost heart. In the ensuing months many died, others moved away, while a growing number used the veneer of education they had acquired in Britain to go into the slave trade on their own account by intimidating the local natives. By the spring of 1788, the whites had gone, and only 130 blacks remained in Granville Town. It came as no surprise when, in 1789, some of the locals, led by one of the chiefs, King Jemmy, sacked the town, and drove the remaining settlers out into the jungle. So ended Granville Sharp's dream of a new African home for freed slaves.

At home, the struggle to outlaw slavery for once and for all went on. William Wilberforce, backed by Prime Minister Pitt, brought before Parliament a bill which proposed the abolition of the slave trade but, as might be expected, he met stiff opposition from those with a vested interest in the trade, many of whom were rich and politically powerful. They produced two convincing arguments in favour of continuing the trade, firstly that the plantations in the colonies could not be profitably worked without the slaves, so threatening the very existence of the British Empire, and secondly that it would mean the end of the merchant fleet, which depended on the trade for much of its employment. And as the Royal Navy relied on the merchant ships to supply a large percentage of their crews, then they too would suffer a crippling loss. In addition, it was argued that Africans taken into slavery, once they had settled down in their new country, were far better off than they had been in their native land, where their existence had been at best barbaric.

The struggle was long and bitter, and was eventually to destroy Wilberforce's health. He persevered, however, and on 16 March

1807, by a majority of 267 votes, Parliament passed the Abolition of the Slave Trade Act.

The last British slaver recorded as being involved in the trade was the *Kitty's Amelia*, commanded by the amiable Captain Hugh Crow. She sailed from Liverpool on 27 July 1807 and, having been cleared from the port before the Act became law, was still able to procure a cargo of slaves in West Africa. When Crow informed his old friend, King Holiday, ruler of Bonny, that the trade was coming to an end, the King replied: 'Crow, you and me sabby each other long time, and me know you tell me true mouth. You king and you big man stop we trade, and s'pose dat true, what we do? For you sabby me have too much child. Suppose some of we child go bad and we no can sell em, we father must kill dem own child; and s'pose trade be done we force kill too much child same way. But we tink trade no stop, for all we Ju Ju man say you country no can niber pass God Almighty.'

Which loosely translated from the pidgin reads: 'Crow, we've known each other for a long time, and I believe what you say. But if your people stop the trade, what will I do? You know I have many subjects, and if some of them commit crimes I will no longer be able to sell them, which means I will have to kill them. But I know the trade will not really stop. All my wise men say that your country can never be above God himself.'

The *Kitty Amelia*'s passage across the Atlantic was dogged by bad fortune. Soon after sailing from Africa, she went to the rescue of another ship that had been wrecked. The survivors were taken on board, but they repaid Crow's generosity by bringing sickness with them which quickly spread to his crew. Later, in mid-Atlantic, fire broke out in the cargo and threatened to spread to the powder magazine. There were forty-five barrels of gunpowder in the magazine, and a catastrophic explosion that would tear the ship apart seemed certain. Panic set in, and the crew were about to take to the boats when Crow prevailed on them to stay aboard and fight the fire, which he then proceeded to smother using the spare set of sails.

On arrival in Kingston, Crow found sixteen other ships at anchor, all with slaves on board which, because of the repercussions of the Act of Abolition, they were unable to sell. However, such was Crow's reputation in the islands that he had no difficulty in making a sale, but this would be his last involvement in the slave trade. He left the *Kitty's Amelia* in Kingston, sending her back to Liverpool with another master in command. He followed later as a passenger in another ship.

The Act finally became fully operative in January 1808, and it was then up to the Royal Navy to police the slave trade and eradicate it. This was all very well, but the Navy had been almost continuously at war for fifteen years. It was then currently fighting France in the Atlantic, the Mediterranean and the Indian Ocean, and at the same time the ships of most other European nations were hostile to it. The battle to banish slavery from the face of the high seas once and for all would be long and bitter.

Chapter Five

Poacher Turned Gamekeeper

Neither mountains, rivers nor deserts will prove barriers to the slave trade, as the black chiefs will bring their slaves from every extremity of Africa as long as there is a nation that will afford them a slave market.

Sir James Yeo, 1816

As on so many occasions in her long history, when the cards were on the table, Britain stood alone on the abolition of the slave trade. There may have been a growing acceptance in mainland Europe and North America that the trade was not quite ethical, but it had flourished for centuries. Most nations could see no good reason to call a halt now. Only little Denmark, having outlawed the trade in 1803, was in agreement with British thinking, but even she was not yet prepared to act. In fact, the mere suggestion that Perfidious Albion, once the chief poacher, had turned gamekeeper, was treated with a great deal of cynicism throughout the world. It was even put around in some quarters that she was acting in her own selfish interests in denying cheap labour to other countries which were in competition with her plantations in the West Indies.

While the politicians had forced through the Act of Abolition, only the Royal Navy could enforce it, and that would entail sending ships to the west coast of Africa, the main source of the slave trade. At any other time the Navy would have set about the job with characteristic enthusiasm, but there were other more pressing commitments. Britain was then actively at war with France and under threat of invasion from across the Channel, where Napoleon's armies were massing. The Royal Navy had 795 ships in commission, but they were very thinly spread. Apart from guarding the Channel, the Navy was engaged in blockading the French Biscay ports, patrolling the Mediterranean, and defending the colonies in the Caribbean and Indian Ocean. If she wished to maintain her maritime supremacy, Britain must continue to show the flag. And this was at a time when there was serious unrest in the ships following the mutiny at the Nore at the turn of the century, which had resulted in twenty-five of the ringleaders being hanged at the yardarm. The lower decks of the Navy had gained precious little from the mutiny, and they continued to simmer.

The Admirals were not pleased when they were given the additional task of suppressing the slave trade, as was evident from their response. After much prevarication two ships were found, the 23-year-old frigate *Solebay*, and the newly built sloop *Derwent*. The *Solebay*, in which Commodore Edward Columbine flew his flag, mounted thirty-two guns, while the *Derwent*, commanded by Lieutenant Frederick Parker, carried just eighteen guns. Both ships were slow and ill-fitted for the chase, and to expect them to effectively police nearly 3000 miles of the coast of West Africa, which was the duty assigned to them, was ambitious to say the least. As for the men who manned the ships, 250 in the *Solebay* and 195 in the *Derwent*, they knew little of the hardships they would face on the coast: the stifling heat, the torrential rains, the flies, mosquitoes and malignant fevers that could run through a ship cutting men down like corn under the scythe. Nor were they aware of the risks they would run should they dare to step ashore in this hostile land, where they would surely face death on a daily basis at the hands of the natives, irate slave traders, snakes, crocodiles, and numerous other ferocious inhabitants of the jungle.

There were some consolations for the men of this grandly named African Squadron. The Act authorised them to seize any pirate vessel or any ship with false or suspect papers, which allowed a great deal of latitude in the taking of prizes. There were also handsome returns for any slaver taken out of business. For every male slave set free a bounty of £60 would be paid, for every female £30, and for every child £10, all to be distributed amongst the officers and crew of the two ships according to the Prize Regulations. The latter stipulated that any bounty paid be divided into eighths, three eighths going to the captain, one eighth to the officers, one eighth to the petty officers, two eighths to the ratings, and the remaining eighth to the commander-in-chief of the station. For those accustomed to earning only a pittance – an able seaman, then being on only thirty shillings a month – the financial attractions offered by service in the African Squadron overcame all the dangers involved.

Solebay and *Derwent* sailed for West Africa early in 1808, and a month later, after calling at Madeira for fresh water and provisions, reached Sierra Leone, now a thriving British colony. Officially, they were part of the Cape Fleet, then stationed at Ascension Island, but Commodore Columbine established his base at Freetown, the newly named capital of Sierra Leone, and began a series of exploratory patrols along the coast. Looking into the apparently endless number of rivers, creeks, inlets and bays that indented the coast, Columbine soon became aware of the extent of the slave trade. The slave ships were everywhere, queuing up in the anchorages to take on their human cargoes. However, the slavers flew the flags of Spain, Portugal, the United States and France, while Columbine was authorised to stop and board only British ships. The latter, it would seem, had either withdrawn from the trade following the passage of the Act of Abolition in London, or were sailing under foreign flags of convenience. The result was that the first patrol of the embryo African Squadron freed no slaves. It did, however, afford Columbine the opportunity of thoroughly exploring the coast and identifying the main centres of the trade. It was not until the summer of 1809, when *Solebay* and *Derwent* were making their way home empty handed – much to the disgust of their bountiless crews – that they were able to make a contribution towards Britain's influence on the coast.

Sailing from the Sierra Leone River on 15 June, the two ships went north in convoy, having with them the gun brig *Tigress*, the transport *Agincourt*, the colonial schooner *George*, and several homeward bound merchantmen. With the advantage of a light following breeze and a favourable current, the convoy reached the Bay of Goree, 500 miles north of Freetown, on the 20th, where the ships called to top up their water butts and stock up with any fresh provisions available.

The arrival of Columbine and his squadron was the answer to a prayer for Major Maxwell, commander of the British garrison on Goree Island. For some months Maxwell had been troubled by French privateers harassing British shipping off Cape Verde, and was unable to put a stop to these attacks. The privateers, he explained to Columbine, were based at St. Louis, on the Senegal River, and to mount an expedition against them overland would entail a 100-mile march through hostile French territory, an undertaking too hazardous to contemplate. In Maxwell's opinion, the only feasible solution was to attack from seaward, and for that he needed Columbine's ships.

In an age when communication between Britain and her far flung outposts of Empire was only as fast as the fastest sailing packet, commanders on the spot were given a great deal of freedom of action. Major Maxwell had the troops and Commodore Columbine had the ships, and between them they devised a plan for an attack on St. Louis. The merchant ships were left at anchor under the guns of Goree Island, and on 4 July *Agincourt*, with Maxwell and 160 men of the Royal Africa Corps on board, escorted by *Solebay, Derwent, Tigress* and the schooner *George*, sailed for St. Louis.

The fleet arrived off the mouth of the Senegal River at dawn on the 7th, and anchored close inshore to await full daylight. Commodore Columbine was not familiar with the river, but his charts and sailing directions, such as they were, warned him that the crossing of the bar would not be an easy operation. The Senegal is one of Africa's greatest rivers, navigable by shallow draught vessels as far as 400 miles inland, but the long sand bar across its mouth is a formidable obstacle. Built up by the reaction between the huge outflow of the river and the big swell that surges in from the Atlantic, the bar stretches for several miles and has only one navigable passage for ocean-going ships. Passe de Gandiole, a channel 400 feet wide, and with a depth of 11 feet, is difficult to discern in the surf constantly breaking on the bar, and any attempt to enter without local knowledge is not wise at the best of times. Columbine had no such help, but if he were to land Maxwell's troops, he had to enter the river.

Agincourt was drawing too much water to be able to cross the bar, so the men of the Royal Africa Corps were disembarked into boats, along with a force of 120 seamen and 50 marines led by Captain Parker, commander of the *Derwent*. With two leadsmen in the chains chanting the depths, the *George* led the way through the Passe de Gandiole, with the pulling boats, escorted by *Solebay*, *Derwent* and *Tigress*, following in her wake.

Crossing the bar was a nail-biting operation, and progress was agonizingly slow, but all went well until a rogue wave swept through the channel, capsizing one of *Derwent*'s boats. Tragically, Captain Frederick Parker, Midshipman Francis Sealy, and six seamen were drowned.

The landing force negotiated the rest of the channel without further mishap, but once inside the river the *George* ran ashore in sight of St. Louis, and could not be refloated. It was just as well that the French garrison, which consisted of 160 regulars and 240 militia, had been taken completely by surprise and retreated further up river on sighting the British ships. Maxwell landed his troops, and took up a defensive position on shore to protect the stranded schooner. The other ships then anchored off St. Louis.

It took two days of hard work in sweltering temperatures to refloat the *George*, this being achieved largely by the efforts of Lieutenant Daniel Woodriff of *Solebay*. On the morning of the 12th, with Lieutenant Joseph Tetley, first lieutenant of the *Solebay*, in command of *Derwent*, the flotilla moved up river. They found the French 12 miles inland at the trading post of Babague, which was heavily defended by a boom stretched across the river. Behind the boom seven armed boats patrolled under the protection of a considerable battery of guns on shore. Commodore Columbine was not deterred. He anchored his ships within gunshot, and *Solebay* and *Derwent* opened fire on the post.

The French had no real stomach for the fight, and before night fell they had hoisted the white flag of surrender. Major Maxwell and his men entered Babague, capturing twenty-eight long 24-pounder guns, four brass mortars and howitzers, and sixteen smaller guns. The surrender was signed on 13 July, Commodore Columbine taking possession of St. Louis and all its dependencies in the name of the British Crown.

For the British the cost of the expedition had been surprisingly small. Apart from the unfortunate deaths of Captain Parker and seven others in his boat, only one officer of the Royal Africa Corps died, as a result of heat stroke, and one soldier was wounded. However, as they left the river the squadron suffered a major blow when the frigate *Solebay* ran aground and became a total loss. Fortunately all her men were taken off safely, and some of her stores were salvaged.

Derwent sailed home alone, taking the *Solebay* men with her, and at a court martial held in Portsmouth on 11 September that year Commodore Edward Columbine, his officers and crew, were found not to blame for the loss of their ship. The court did, however, find that the night before *Solebay* ran aground four of her seamen, Michael Grace, Thomas Jones, Charles Nileus and Robert Storks, were 'in a state of drunkenness'. Whether this had any bearing on the loss of the frigate was not decided. For their 'inexcusable dereliction of duty', Grace and Jones received 150 lashes, and Nileus and Storks 50 lashes each. At another court martial, held on the following day, John Ashley, the *Derwent*'s carpenter, was found guilty of being so drunk on the day of the attack on the French at Barbague that he was unable to lead his men into action. He was dismissed the Service and sentenced to six months in the notorious naval gaol at Marshalsea.

And so ended the brief life of the Royal Navy's first African Squadron, which had achieved little except to show good intentions – at least this was the perception. But with the *Solebay* lost and the *Derwent* back on patrol in the Channel, it became evident that their presence on the West African coast had not been entirely without effect on the slave trade. In the autumn of 1809 reports began to come in from Sierra Leone that there had been a substantial increase in the number of slavers operating on the coast, many of them sailing under the Spanish flag. There was a reason for the sudden influx of so-called Spanish ships into the trade. Theoretically the United States of America had come into line with Britain and outlawed the carriage of slaves in its ships on January 1808; in reality, all the Americans had done was to re-register their vessels under the Spanish flag. The legal niceties were taken care of by sending a ship to the Canary Islands or Cuba, where a sale was made on paper to a Spanish buyer, and a Spanish master was appointed to command. The ship was then to all intents and purposes Spanish, and as Spain had not yet outlawed the slave trade, she was free to carry the black cargoes so urgently needed to maintain production on the American plantations. The original crew remained with the ship, as did the American captain who, when the need arose, posed as a supercargo or a passenger, while the Spanish captain dealt with any inquisitive boarders. It was a neat arrangement, and as maritime law then stood, perfectly legal.

The demands made on British naval forces by the war with France were so great that no more ships could be spared for West Africa, and it was not until 1811, when the pressure began to ease, that the Admiralty saw fit to re-form the African Squadron. This time the squadron was a more realistic proposition. In command was Captain Frederick Irby, a man of considerable experience, who had fought at Camperdown and the Glorious First of June under Admiral Adam Duncan. Irby flew his flag in the 38-gun frigate *Amelia*, a fifth-rate ship taken from the French off the south of Ireland in 1796. She was a stoutly built, handy ship, capable of speeds up to 12 knots with a favourable wind. *Amelia* was supported by the *Ganymede*, a 24-gun brig, also a prize taken from the French, commanded by Captain Robert Preston. Two sloops, the *Trinculo* of 18 guns, commanded by Captain Alex Renny, and the *Kangaroo*, with Captain John Lloyd in command, completed the squadron.

Irby arrived off Sierra Leone in the autumn of 1811, his orders being to patrol the coast from Cape Verde to Benguela, a 2,600-mile-long beat stretching across the Equator from 12° North to 15° South. This was clearly an impossible assignment for four small ships, so Irby decided from the outset that he would confine his activities to the coast between Isle de Los, which lies 80 miles north of Freetown, and the Portuguese island of St. Thomas, or São Tomé, at the southern end of the Gulf of Guinea. Even this seemed ambitious, since for most of the year this coast is almost entirely within the Doldrums. In the calms and light, fitful winds of the area even a fast craft like the *Amelia* would be reduced to endless tacking to and fro to fill her sails. The prevailing wind – when it blew – was in the south-west, and the current set from east to west, so that although running south from Freetown was difficult, but possible, returning up the coast was an excruciatingly slow business. At the same time, navigation was very much a hit and miss affair. Charts and sailing directions were mostly inaccurate or vague, the coast was low-lying and often obscured by haze, and with a steeply shelving shore, the lead gave very little warning of danger. Adding to all those difficulties was the hot, humid climate of West Africa which, even today, in air-conditioned ships, is trying. For Irby's men, in their crowded, badly ventilated ships, on a monotonous diet of rancid salt meat and stale ship's biscuit, life must have resembled purgatory afloat. But such inconveniences paled into insignificance against the dreadful tropical diseases that assailed them, of which malaria and yellow fever, or the black vomit as it was popularly called, were top of the list.

Captain Irby had been given the authority to stop and search all ships suspected of being involved in the slave trade, especially those of Spain, Portugal and the United States, these being the main culprits. The punishment for carrying slaves in a British ship was transportation for fourteen years, so he assumed there would be no necessity to harass his own ships. However, Irby soon discovered that a number of British ships were sailing under a foreign flag, mainly that of Spain. Not only were they flying a false flag, but they frequently used Spanish names and ports of registration, all of which indicated the vast profits to be made in slaving.

Within weeks of arriving on the coast, Irby's squadron was boarding, arresting, and sending ships back to Freetown, where an Admiralty Prize Court had been set up. The ships were usually burnt or sold off and the slaves taken under the wing of local authority. After a year in Freetown these freed slaves were given the option of volunteering to be shipped to the British West Indies as bonded labourers, or being allowed to go free in the colony and fend for themselves. The majority of freed slaves opted to stay in Sierra Leone, and at times their presence threatened to undermine the stability of the region.

At the end of December 1811 Irby was lying at anchor off Freetown when he received word that forty-five Portuguese ships were loading slaves on the coast between Cape Palmas and Calabar. Ordering Captain Lloyd to follow him in *Kangaroo* as soon as she was ready for sea, Irby took *Amelia* out of Freetown harbour and sailed east. Within a few days of leaving, he had stopped and seized the Portuguese brig *São João*, loaded with a full cargo of slaves, and sent her back with a prize crew on board to be dealt with by the court at Freetown. Further along the coast he boarded the brig *Bom Caminho*, also under the Portuguese flag. Equipment found on board left Irby in no doubt that she was a slaver, but as she had not yet loaded her slaves, he was obliged to let her go. Both Portuguese ships stopped were armed, but faced by *Amelia*'s formidable array of long 18-pounders, 12-pounders and 32-pound carronades, they had offered no resistance.

The *Kangaroo* left Freetown on 8 January 1812, hoping to meet up with the *Amelia* either at Cape Coast Castle or, failing that, off St. Thomas. Unexpectedly, Lloyd ran into an area of calms, and the sloop spent day after day drifting aimlessly, her sails hanging limp. It was the 24th of the month before she reached Cape Coast Castle, having made good an average speed of only 2 knots. By the time *Kangaroo* anchored off the fort, *Amelia* had gone on her way. After a brief stop to gather intelligence and take on fresh water, Lloyd followed Irby down the coast, but once again he ran into light, variable winds, and the long haul south to St. Thomas was frustratingly slow. *Kangaroo* finally came to anchor off St. Thomas on 16 February, nearly six weeks after sailing from Freetown. Once again Lloyd had missed his rendezvous with Irby, *Amelia* having already left for Freetown. This left Lloyd free to act on his own initiative and he decided to remain in the area for a few days in the hope of flushing out a slaver or two.

The first opportunity for action came sooner than Lloyd expected. On the morning of the 21st, when *Kangaroo* was lying at anchor off the north-east corner of St. Thomas, a cutter under full sail was sighted to the east. The stranger was very low in the water, leading Captain Lloyd to suspect that her cargo might bear investigation. He hove short his anchor preparatory to getting under way, but as *Kangaroo* was in the lee of the island, there was not enough wind even to take the creases out of her sails. For the next hour and a half Lloyd was forced to watch and fume as the cutter sailed past and pulled away. Fortunately, before she reached the far horizon, a westerly breeze sprang up, and *Kangaroo* was able to get under way at last.

The British ship was a fast sailer with the wind abaft the beam, and within the hour she had the cutter within range of her guns. Lloyd put a shot across her bows and signalled her to heave to, but the cutter's only reply was to hoist more sail. A second shot was fired, but this also brought no response, and the chase went on for another half an hour before, using round shot and musket fire, *Kangaroo* forced the cutter to lower her sails.

A boat was sent across with an armed boarding party, which confirmed Lloyd's suspicions regarding the cutter. She was Portuguese, and had a total of sixty-three slaves hidden below deck. Her master claimed he had loaded the slaves in the neighbouring Princes Island and was taking them direct to Brazil, which to Lloyd seemed a highly unlikely proposition in such a small craft. He inclined towards the opinion that the cutter was on a coastal voyage, ferrying the slaves to a brig he had earlier seen anchored close in to St. Thomas. He decided to arrest the cutter and her crew. A prize crew led by *Kangaroo*'s master's mate, was put on board with orders to take the cutter and her cargo of slaves to Freetown, where the Prize Court would rule on their fate.

Having sent the Portuguese cutter away, Lloyd decided to try his luck further to the east, and *Kangaroo* arrived off the mainland, near the mouth of the Gabon River, on the morning of 28 February. Once anchored, a boat was sent ashore, which soon returned with the news that a brig was reported to be loading slaves up river. As soon as the boat was hoisted aboard, Lloyd weighed anchor and entered the river. *Kangaroo* grounded when crossing the bar, but the wind was fresh and she was carrying sufficient sail to take her over into deep water. By 11.30 she was safely anchored in 6½ fathoms in the broad estuary of the Gabon with a good view up river for several miles. There was no sign of the slaver, and Lloyd assumed she must be hidden around a bend in the river.

Like most of Africa's great rivers, the Gabon was navigable by ocean-going ships well inland, but not having local knowledge, and having already run aground once, Captain Lloyd was not inclined to venture further. That afternoon *Kangaroo*'s pinnace and cutter were sent away, manned by armed seamen and marines, with orders to find and seize the slaver.

Next morning, those remaining on board *Kangaroo* were

surprised to see a schooner come down river and anchor alongside them. She had been found up river, boarded by the *Kangaroo*'s men, and arrested on suspicion of slaving. However, close examination of the prize revealed no evidence that she was involved, and Lloyd had no alternative but to let her go. Nor did he have any success with the brig he was looking for. His boats returned next morning, having been unable to find any trace of the ship. It was a somewhat dispirited Lloyd who later that day sailed out of the Gabon River to return to Freetown. *Kangaroo* had been seven weeks at sea, covered around 1,500 miles, and had nothing to show for it except one cutter arrested and sixty-three slaves freed.

On 28 March, when passing Cape Coast Castle on his way back to the west, Lloyd came across the London schooner *Quiz*. She ran away when the *Kangaroo* approached, but the sloop had several knots on her, and the chase was brief. When boarded, the *Quiz* was found to be a British privateer armed with a letter of marque from the Governor of Sierra Leone authorising her master to seize any vessel he found to be engaged in slaving. Lloyd had not been informed of this unorthodox supplement to the African Squadron, and he was not happy that his authority in the area was being undermined by a mere merchant ship. The only good thing to come out of the meeting of the two ships was that the master of the schooner informed Lloyd that a number of slavers had been seen at Whydah, a trading post some 300 miles to the east. Although it meant retracing his steps, Lloyd decided to investigate.

Kangaroo arrived off Whydah on the morning of 5 April, where she found no fewer than six Portuguese brigs at anchor. It was just possible that they were ordinary merchantmen going about their normal business, but this was highly unlikely. The Portuguese were among the leaders in the slave trade, and Whydah was one of their regular ports of call. As soon as his anchor was down, Lloyd sent a boat away to board the nearest brig. As the boat approached, there was a flurry of activity aboard the brig that bordered on panic, and the Portuguese were seen to abandon ship and row frantically for the shore. When *Kangaroo*'s boarding party reached the deck of the brig, now identified as the *Uranus*, a bizarre sight greeted them. The sole occupants of the ship were five British seamen, some of them in irons. They were, it was revealed, a prize crew put aboard by the privateer *Quiz*, and subsequently overpowered by the *Uranus*'s crew. Questioned by Captain Lloyd, the rescued men related that a few days earlier the *Quiz* had come into the anchorage under the British flag, lowered this, hoisted the Jolly Roger, and then mounted an attack on the slavers. She had succeeded in taking the *Uranus*, but the other brigs had driven her off with gunfire.

Lloyd boarded the Portuguese ships, finding them all without cargo, except one which had 130 slaves hidden in her hold. The others protested their innocence, but Lloyd suspected they were awaiting the arrival of their slaves, and that had he arrived a few days later it would have been a different story. As it was, he was only able to arrest the one vessel that had slaves on board. He escorted this ship and the *Uranus* back to Freetown.

Kangaroo and her prizes arrived in Freetown on 16 May, a disappointed Lloyd reporting to Captain Irby that all he had to show for a gruelling cruise lasting four months was a cutter and two brigs captured, and 193 slaves freed. Clearly, the British African Squadron would need to be considerably enlarged if it was to make any impression on the West African slave trade, which seemed to be flourishing despite the Act of Abolition. Britain still stood alone in her fight to stamp out this abomination.

Things took a turn for the worse when on 18 June that year the United States of America, incensed by the Royal Navy's interference with her Atlantic shipping, declared war on Britain. For the Navy, hard-pressed on so many other fronts, this could well prove to be the straw that broke the proverbial camel's back. The American navy was small, but it was well manned, and included a number of first-class frigates quite able to do battle with the Royal Navy's best, and win. The first to be on the receiving end of the guns of the embryo US Navy was His Majesty's ship *Java*.

The 38-gun frigate *Java*, commanded by Captain Henry Lambert, sailed from Spithead on 12 November 1812 with two East Indiamen. The Company's ships, one of which had on board the new Commander-in-Chief India and his staff, were bound for Bombay. *Java* was also acting as a transport, carrying a large quantity of naval stores for the Indian port. Making the best of the prevailing winds, the three ships followed the well-trodden path down the Atlantic towards the coast of Brazil, where they hoped to pick up the westerly-blowing anti-trades for the Cape of Good Hope.

A month out of the Channel and passing to the west of the Cape Verde Islands, the convoy met an American merchant ship, which the *Java* chased and took as a prize. Captain Lambert was to regret indulging in this diversion, for in order to make up a prize crew for the American, he robbed his own ship of many of her most experienced seamen. This left the *Java* with a complement of 272 on board, of which all but fifty were raw hands on their first voyage to sea.

As December drew to a close, the convoy was approaching the coast of Brazil, but *Java*, which carried a larger crew than the Indiamen, was beginning to run dangerously short of fresh water. On the 24th, assuming that there was little prospect of meeting hostile ships in these waters, Lambert decided to leave his charges to look after themselves, and take *Java* into the nearest Brazilian port, San Salvador, to refill her water casks.

Cramming on all sail, Lambert sighted the Brazilian coast on the 29th, confident now that he would soon be able to rejoin the convoy. But that morning what appeared to be a merchant ship flying the United States flag was sighted, and once again Henry Lambert was tempted. He gave chase.

Java was a powerful ship, mounting twenty-eight long 18-pounders on the main deck, sixteen 32-pounder carronades on the quarterdeck, and two long 9-pounders on the forecastle head. She was, however, in the hands of a depleted and largely inexperienced crew and Lambert should not have chosen to pick a fight with an unknown enemy. This enemy proved to be the 44-gun frigate USS *Constitution*. In command was Commodore William Bainbridge, who had with him a complement of 480, many of whom were British, and all of whom were experienced men. The *Constitution*, affectionately known in the US Navy as 'Old Ironsides' due to her stout and apparently shot-proof hull, was more than ready to give battle.

The two ships were within gunshot range by early afternoon, and having hoisted her American colours, the *Constitution* fired the first broadside. *Java* replied, and then, at a range of half a mile, the two frigates fought it out broadside for broadside. Soon a thick pall of gunsmoke lay over the sea, penetrated by orange tongues of flame as the opposing gun captains urged their sweating crews to load and fire ever faster. A lucky hit early on damaged the American's steering gear, but her superior firepower and accurate shooting soon began to inflict serious damage and casualties on the *Java*. Half an hour later, both her main and mizzen topmasts had gone, and Captain Henry Lambert lay seriously wounded on his quarterdeck.

Java's First Lieutenant, Lieutenant Henry Chads, now assumed command. He was determined to continue the fight, but the odds were too great. Most of the British frigate's guns were out of action, thirty-one of her crew lay dead, and over a hundred others were wounded. Under the devastating broadsides still being fired by the *Constitution*, Chads was forced to accept defeat. He struck his colours.

Commodore Bainbridge, himself wounded, showed compassion for his defeated foes, landing them in Salvador three days later. There, Captain Henry Lambert died of his wounds and was buried with full naval honours on 5 January. Lieutenant Chads and the other survivors gave their parole, and were put aboard two small ships flying a flag of truce to be returned to England. Two months later, in the approaches to the English Channel, the ships were chased and boarded by the French frigate *Arethuse*, and for the second time in the space of a month the *Java*'s men were made prisoners of war.

Henry Chads was taken aboard the *Arethuse*, where he observed that the frigate had suffered very heavy damage in a fight. Her lower masts, fore and main yards, gaff, spanker boom and mizzen topmast were all fractured and supported by splints, and there were more than thirty round shot still lodged in her hull. From papers he saw in the frigate's cabin Chads ascertained that she had suffered thirty-one killed and seventy-four wounded in the battle, which was with none other than Captain Frederick Irby's *Amelia*.

By the end of December 1812 HMS *Amelia* had spent more than twelve months on the West African station, and was suffering badly from the ravages of the coast. Her hull was foul with barnacles and weed, her sails threadbare, many of her men were down with fever, and she bore the scars of dozens of encounters with belligerent slavers. She was about to return to Portsmouth for a refit when, on 27 January 1813, Lieutenant William Pascoe and his crew arrived in Freetown to report the loss of their brig HMS *Daring*, which had been burned by the French off the Isle de Los. Irby acted immediately.

Lieutenant Pascoe was sent back to the Isle de Los in the government schooner *Princess Charlotte* with instructions to gain intelligence on the current situation. He returned to Freetown on 4 February to report that the French frigates *Arethuse* and *Rubis* were still off the islands, and obviously intent on attacking British shipping. Captain Irby then replaced the sick members of his crew with men from the *Daring* and set sail for the north in *Amelia*. Lieutenant Pasoce went with him.

Arriving off the Isle de Los on the 6 February, Irby found the French frigates anchored, some distance apart, off Tamara Island. Unknown to the British captain, the southernmost of the two enemy ships, the *Rubis*, was in fact hard and fast on a rock. As soon as *Amelia* hove in sight, the *Arethuse* weighed anchor and put to sea ready to do battle. The French frigate, commanded by Captain Bouvet, mounted twenty-eight 18-pounders on the main deck and sixteen 36-pounder carronades and two long 9-pounder guns on the upper deck. She was a good match for *Amelia*.

Irby accepted the challenge, and for the next four hours the two frigates fought a fierce running battle. The French were firing high, and *Amelia*'s sails and rigging were soon cut to pieces, but although she had lost speed, she fought on. Twice Bouvet put *Arethuse* alongside and tried to board the British ship, but his men were beaten back by the defenders led by Lieutenant Simpson. *Amelia*'s gunners, as later noted by Lieutenant Chads of the *Java*, gave a good account of themselves. Eventually the two evenly matched foes fought themselves to a standstill. *Arethuse* then took the opportunity to break off the fight and escape. *Amelia*, her sailing capacity seriously handicapped, was unable to give chase.

The British ship was left to lick her wounds – and they were grievous. She had lost a total of forty-six killed, including Lieutenant William Pascoe and Marines William Marshall and Peter Bartlett of HMS *Daring*. Five others later died of their wounds, while fifty-one were seriously wounded and forty-four slightly wounded. When the dead had been buried, *Amelia* limped north to Madeira, where temporary repairs were carried out. She paid off in Portsmouth in May 1813, thus bringing to a close another bloody chapter in the history of the African Squadron.

Chapter Six

Rio Pongas

It is only by great cunning (or great accident) that they can be surprised with slaves on board. In some instances, while the boats have been rowing to the slave vessel, the relanding of the slaves has been affected, and then paraded upon the beach, compelled to dance and make every sign of contempt for the boats' crews which the ignorance and brutality of the slave factors or masters could suggest.

Sir George Collier, 1820

By November 1819, the war with France having been over for four years, the Royal Navy at last had ships to spare. In consequence, the African Squadron, now led by Commodore Sir George Collier, who had fought under Nelson at the Battle of the Nile, had been increased to six ships. The enlarged squadron comprised the 36-gun brig *Tartar*, the sloops *Pheasant* (22 guns), *Myrmidon* (20 guns) and *Morgiana* (18 guns), and the 12-gun brigs *Snapper* and *Thistle*. On paper, this was a formidable force, but Collier's ships were in reality only the leavings of the Napoleonic Wars. They were old ships overdue for the breaker's yard, too slow, and still carrying the tall masts that were visible far inland, giving ample warning of their approach. Lord Palmerston, the plain-speaking British statesman, was scathing in his criticism of the Admiralty's continued lack of enthusiasm for tackling the slave trade: 'If there was a particularly old, slow-moving tub in the navy she was sure to be sent to the coast of Africa to try and catch the fast-sailing American clippers.' Nevertheless, this was a considerable improvement on Irby's force but, bearing in mind the complexity and length of coastline

63

Collier was expected to police, its numbers were still woefully inadequate. As before, Collier would able to do little more than show the flag and attempt to blockade the coast. Yet London seemed to think the situation in West Africa was well under control. A more realistic picture was painted by the following, which appeared in *The Times* of 7 April 1820:

> Extract of letter from Sierra Leone, dated December 14 1819:- There are no less than seven slave-vessels now in the Rio Pongas, and an equal number were lately in the Rio Numez. The neighbouring rivers have also a large portion of this abominable trade. There are three slave prizes now lying at Sierra Leone for adjudication; and we have a report that one of his Majesty's vessels on the Leeward station has already detained 13 slave-vessels. I know the coast perfectly well, and do not hesitate to say that there is now (at the close of the year 1819) more slave-trading carried on than when it was allowed by the British Government: yet to read accounts from the Sierra Leone Gazette, you would suppose the slave-trade nearly destroyed, the slaves perfectly happy and free, and that we were living in the most salubrious climate on earth: but those accounts are fabricated for the benefit of persons on your side of the water, who direct every thing relating to this canting and deleterious colony.

The reality was that, although British ships had withdrawn from the trade since Abolition in 1807, the French, Spanish, Portuguese and Americans – all of whom had by this time officially agreed to outlaw slave traffic – were still as actively engaged in the trade as ever.

That part of the African coast that stretches between the River Gambia and Sierra Leone is flat and low-lying, deeply indented by numerous creeks and rivers that flow into the Atlantic between banks covered with thick, lush mangroves. The principal rivers are the Rio Nunez, Rio Compony, Rio Pongas, and Rio Mellacoree, and of these the Rio Pongas played the most important role in the assembly and shipping of slaves. Its estuary is a veritable labyrinth of secret creeks and streams, through which canoes can slip effortlessly and unseen, while its seaward entrances are guarded by sandbanks that shift with every change of tide. There were then only two deep-water channels, each with a minimum depth of three fathoms, but with currents that were fast running and unpredictable. It was a foolish navigator who attempted to enter the Rio Pongas without the help of a pilot.

In May 1820 the 12-gun brig HMS *Thistle*, commanded by Lieutenant Robert Hagan, was on patrol duty in the vicinity of the Rio Pongas. On 5 May, having sighted nothing of interest for several days, Hagan called at the Isle de Los, where a British trading post had been established, to seek news of movements on the coast. While the brig was at anchor, a merchant named Proctor boarded to complain that one of his ships had been taken by pirates in the Rio Pongas. He named the ringleader of the pirates as one Thomas Curtis, who was known to Lieutenant Hagan. Curtis, born in the British colony of Massachusetts in 1774 of a British father and a black mother, had been trading in the area since 1815. He was a powerful man on the Rio Pongas, and while he had never been convicted, it was common knowledge that he was deeply involved in the slave trade.

Robert Hagan, who had served for five years on the coast, four of them in an armed brig of the Sierra Leone government, was very familiar with the Rio Pongas, and as Proctor was willing to accompany him, he felt confident of being able to rescue the captured ship.

Thistle arrived off the entrance to the Rio Pongas at dawn on 6 May, but due to the state of the tide was unable to cross the bar into the river. Hagan anchored off and sent a boat in to deliver a letter to Curtis demanding the release of Proctor's ship. The boat was under the command of Midshipman Robert Inman.

After crossing the bar Inman and his boat's crew faced a long pull up river to the village of Boffa, where it was believed Thomas Curtis had his landing stage. On the way they came across Proctor's ship anchored in a wide stretch of the river some 5 miles below Boffa. Although Lieutenant Hagan's explicit orders were to deliver the letter to Curtis and return to the *Thistle* at once, young Inman could not resist the temptation to board the anchored ship and take possession of her. But before he could carry out his intentions his boat came under heavy musket fire from the river bank, where men were hidden in the thick mangroves. In the hail of bullets, Robert Inman and several of his men were killed, and others wounded. The boat drifted into the bank, and those of the crew still alive were taken captive by Curtis's men, who had set up the ambush.

The firing was heard on board the *Thistle*, anchored outside the river mouth, but there was little Hagan could do. Crossing the bar without a pilot would almost certainly lead to the ship running aground, and that would achieve nothing. Likewise, opening fire with his guns on an unseen target ashore would serve no useful purpose. When news reached him of Inman's fate and the capture of his surviving crew, Lieutenant Hagan decided that the best course of action was to weigh anchor and make all sail for Freetown to get help in rescuing his men.

On arrival at Freetown, 120 miles to the south, Hagan found that Commodore Collier was away from the station with *Tartar*. He therefore reported to the senior naval officer present, Captain Henry Leeke, who commanded the sloop *Myrmidon*. Leeke took Hagan to see the governor, Lieutenant-Colonel Charles Macarthy, and pressed for an expedition to be mounted to rescue the missing men and bring the pirates to book. Macarthy pleaded that this was a matter for the Navy, and with the commodore absent he was loath to act. Leeke, in turn, pointed out that every hour lost brought greater danger to the *Thistle*'s men in Curtis's hands, and insisted that action be taken. After further prevarication, Macarthy finally agreed.

In Freetown, Captain Leeke had at his disposal the *Myrmidon*, Hagan's *Thistle*, the sloop *Morgiana*, and the small brig *Snapper*. This was hardly a large force, but as they mounted a total of sixty-two guns between them, he was satisfied the ships would do the job. Lieutenant-Colonel Macarthy offered three companies of the 2nd West India Regiment, 150 men and 4 officers, under the command of Captain James Chisholm.

Captain Chisholm and his men embarked aboard *Myrmidon* and *Morgiana* on 10 May, just as Commodore Sir George Collier returned in HMS *Tartar*. After some discussion Collier approved the operation, and the little fleet sailed on the morning of the 12th. Leeke had placed all his marines under Chisholm's command, and the combined landing force was to enter the Rio Pongas in boats provided by the four ships. Chisholm's orders from the governor were to recover the prisoners and to take

Thomas Curtis into custody. He was to fire only when fired on, and there was to be no wanton plundering and burning of the African villages. With an eye to the future, Macarthy and Collier were anxious not to upset the local chiefs.

In light winds, and sailing against the run of the current, the squadron arrived off the Rio Pongas before dawn on the 15th. At first light the ships came to anchor off the main entrance to the river, and within sight of the continuous line of breakers marking the bar. As there was only a depth of 16 feet on the bar at high water, Leeke decided that the bigger ships, *Myrmidon* and *Morgiana*, must remain outside, while *Thistle* and *Snapper* entered the river with the landing party on board. The rest of the day was spent transferring the men of the 2nd West India Regiment and the marines, 300 men in all, along with their boats, to the two brigs. It was a difficult operation, but was accomplished without serious incident by the time the sun went down that evening. Captain Leeke then transferred to *Snapper* to take overall command of the landings, and the brigs moved closer in to the bar, anchoring in 3½ fathoms at around 7.30. The two ships were then in a good position for an early start next morning, but they were also in the groundswell, and constantly rolling and tugging at their anchor cables. All on board, particularly the troops packed like sheep on the open decks, spent a very uncomfortable night.

The 16th dawned bright and clear, the line of low sandstone hills inland from the Rio Pongas hardening as the sun climbed behind them, and the pall of low-lying mist over the river slowly dissipated. The wind was light, from the south-south-east: ideal conditions for the task ahead. Anchors were hove short, and as soon as there was sufficient light *Thistle* and *Snapper* weighed and stood in for the entrance, with Lieutenant Hagan, the only officer with any knowledge of the river, leading in *Thistle*. For the run in Hagan lined up a conical-shaped hill, some 6 miles or so inland, with the edge of a sandy beach on the south bank, poor leading marks under the best of circumstances, and doubly so since the current was setting obliquely across the deep-water channel. Throughout, Captain Leeke stood silent on *Snapper*'s quarterdeck, gripping the rail until his knuckles showed white, willing Hagan's judgement to be right.

Hagan's rough and ready navigation was good enough to get the two ships through the gap in the breakers, and once over the bar they moved up river with leadsmen sounding the bottom and lookouts aloft to warn of hidden dangers. The tide was making nicely, and the brigs were in 3 fathoms of water as they passed midway between Observation Point and Marara Island. It might have been prudent to anchor there, where there was sufficient room for both ships to swing, but Leeke was anxious to move as far up river as was possible in order to lessen the distance Chisholm's heavily-loaded boats would have to row.

Hagan moved over to the eastern side of the river, where the deepest water lay, and then led the way through the narrow channel between Big Island and the bank. Carried on the flood tide, with just sufficient sail set to maintain steerage way, the brigs glided past the mangrove-covered banks, moving slowly up river. The silence was eerie, broken only by the frightened screeching of monkeys as they took refuge inland and the occasional hollow plop as a basking crocodile slid into the muddy waters. It was a strange, almost unnerving experience that had those on deck conversing in whispers, as if fearful that the enemy was listening. The troops, crouching behind the bulwarks, gripped their muskets and sweated as the sun climbed high and beat down on their backs.

Clearing Big Island in mid-afternoon, the brigs re-entered a broad stretch of water and found a good anchorage about a mile upstream of the island. They were still 8 miles below the village of Bangalang, where Curtis was thought to have his headquarters, but Leeke decided to go no further until contact had been made with the local chiefs. He wrote the following letter:

To Chiefs and Traders of the Rio Pongas.

The Commanding Officers of His Britannic Majesty's Land and Sea Forces in the Rio Pongas promise upon their most sacred words of honour that they will guarantee the protection and safety of the persons of the many Chiefs of this Country, as will immediately show a disposition to meet them on board one of His Majesty's ships, now in this River for the purpose of bringing to a speedy conclusion the misunderstanding between His Majesty the King of Great Britain and the persons concerned in the late atrocious attack upon the Boat of His Majesty's Brig *Thistle*.

Given under our hands on board His Majesty's Brig *Snapper* in the Rio Pongas 16th May 1820.

Signed   Henry J. Leeke
   Captain of HMS *Myrmidon* and Senior Officer
   of His Majesty's vessels in the Rio Pongas.

Signed   James Chisholm
   Commanding Officer, Capt. 2nd WI Regt.
   of His Majesty's Land Forces.

A passing fishing canoe was called alongside, and its occupants were persuaded, with the aid of a generous bribe of tobacco, to deliver the letter to a British trader called Wilson, who was known to be in Bangalang.

The day wore on. Nothing moved in the river as the ships swung slowly to the turn of the tide and the sun climbed to its zenith before beginning its long descent into the west. The troops checked and re-checked their weapons and equipment, seamen busied themselves around the decks. Everyone fretted. Then, as the sun neared the horizon, and the shadows lengthened, a canoe was seen paddling downstream towards them. The letters it bore were not encouraging. The first was from a trader residing in Bangalang named John Ormond, and read:

To the Commanding Officers of His Britannic Majesty's Sea & Land Forces in the Rio Pongas.

Sirs/

Yours I have just received thro the hand of Mr Wilson, have only to say that it is out of my power to appear on board agreeable to your wish, in consequence of having protected the Four men, which made the escape from Curtis. I must be as present in my house in case Curtis would take the men from me (the letter of which you will receive inclosed). I hope you are informed that I have no animosity against the British Government, and so assure you that there is no persons in my

69

quarter that is ill disposed towards you – I hope you will excuse me from making my appearance according to your request, for the four Men that is now under my protection is at your command whenever you please.

Remain Gentlemen,   Thursday Afternoon
yours friendly   May 17th 1820
John Ormond

The enclosure, dated 12 May, and addressed to John Ormond, read:

Sir/

By the bearer I expect you will deliver the four which I understand are in your possession. I want no further hesitation than their immediate release, as I wish no dispute with you, but in the case of your refusal expect what just deserts merit. Further, you need not expect to clear yourself of other's actions, look back to your own and reflect the detention of these men will be sufficient to evade former actions you are best able to judge, I can't conclude without reminding you of your temerity and unfriendly behaviour in the affair, and again, compliance to my former desire is immediately requested.

Signed

Thomas G. Curtis

Leeke and Chisholm were baffled by the letters. They knew nothing of John Ormond, and questioned whether he really existed. It could well be that they were being invited to walk into a trap. They decided to wait until morning, hoping a reply might come from Wilson, whom they trusted.

Dawn on the 17th was accompanied by a thick haze on the river, and as there had been no communication from Wilson, Leeke decided to move further up river. There was not a breath of wind to fill the sails, so the boats were lowered and began towing the brigs. The procession moved slowly inland, the boats on their long towing hawsers lost in the mist ahead of their tows, their presence revealed only by the muffled creak of rowlocks as the crews bent their backs to their oars. The mist was dense but low-lying, and men posted in the crosstrees of the brigs could see clearly the tops of the trees on either bank. Conditions were perfect for a stealthy approach, but they would not remain that way for long. As soon as the sun was clear of the horizon its heat began to burn off the mist to reveal an empty river, the lush green banks closing in on them as it narrowed.

Soon after 9 o'clock, after towing for more than three hours, Leeke reluctantly concluded that he had brought his ships as far up river as he dared. By then they were in sight of a village which he believed to be Curtis Town, the lair of the man behind the kidnapping of *Thistle*'s men. The brigs were tied up to the east bank of the river, and the boats brought back alongside. Carronades were then lowered over the side and set up in the bows of the leading boats, and Chisholm's force of 170 soldiers and marines boarded, the sun glinting on the 17-inch bayonets of their slung muskets. Captain Leeke had planned to go with them, but his long glass had revealed a mud fort on a hill above Curtis Town. The fort mounted several large guns which covered all possible landing places, and would need to be dealt with by the brigs' guns.

The longboats set off for the shore under a white flag. Chisholm was not sure if the locals were familiar with a flag of truce, but he hoped that the approach of such a large armed party would be enough to persuade them of the need to negotiate. His sole aim was to secure the release of *Thistle*'s men, but if the natives could be prevailed upon to hand over Curtis as well, so much the better. If this could be done without shots being fired, then the day would be won with honour intact on both sides.

It soon became clear that someone on shore understood the flag of truce, for as the boats crept towards the village a large white flag was hoisted over the fort. Chisholm heaved a sigh of relief and ordered the boats to steer for a strip of white sand just below the village. His relief was short-lived, however, for as they neared the beach they came under heavy musket fire from the fort and from marksmen concealed in the mangroves. The boats returned the fire and stood on.

This was the signal Leeke had been waiting for. He ordered *Snapper* and *Thistle* to open fire, and both hurled broadsides at the town and its fort. Under the cover of the ships' guns the boats grounded on the sandy beach, and Chisholm led his men ashore. Crashing through the shallows with their heavy equipment, the troops stormed up the beach, reaching cover in front of the town without suffering a single casualty.

Anxious to consolidate his advantage, Chisholm led his men on, only to discover that the enemy had erected a wooden palisade across the approaches to Curtis Town, from behind which they were laying down a withering fire. Chisholm now had two choices: to dig in and lay siege to the town, or assault the palisade without delay. He chose the latter, advancing slowly, making use of every bit of cover available. This determined attack brought quick results, the enemy melting away before the threat of fixed bayonets and disappearing into the town. Meanwhile, *Snapper* and *Thistle* continued to concentrate their fire on the fort.

Breaking through the palisade, Chisholm sent in skirmishers, who found both the town and the fort on the hill deserted. The enemy could be seen disappearing into the thick bush at the back of the town. Chisholm quickly occupied the town and then approached the bush, calling out to the unseen enemy that he was prepared to offer them safe conduct if they were prepared to palaver. His offer was greeted with a hail of bullets.

Advised that the town had been secured, Captain Leeke came ashore to assess the situation. After consulting with Chisholm, he decided to destroy the palisade, burn all the houses, and raze the fort to the ground, removing all its guns to the ships. It was hoped that this display of force would encourage Curtis, or at least one of his henchmen, to agree to talks. The destruction complete, Chisholm again tried to coax the hidden gunmen out of the bush. This time there was no reply.

The day was now wearing on, and Chisholm was of the opinion that, rather than risk a night action with what appeared to be a vastly superior force, it would be advisable to return to the ships for the night. Remaining ashore after dark would also put the men at risk from the many fevers that infested this fetid jungle. Leeke agreed, and having set fire to a group of houses outside the palisade, the landing party retreated to the boats and put off for the ships.

All were safely back on board by 4 o'clock that afternoon, and soon afterwards a canoe came alongside *Snapper* carrying the trader Wilson, to whom Leeke's letter of the 16th had been delivered. Wilson, who was known and trusted by Leeke, told the two commanders that a powerful local chief, Mongo Braima, who lived about 4 miles up river from Curtis Town, was the real villain of the piece. It was the chief rather than Thomas Curtis, Wilson explained, who had been responsible for the attack on *Thistle*'s boat and the murder of Midshipman Inman and his men. Furthermore, he went on, Mongo Braima was holding captive the survivors of Inman's party. Leeke and Chisholm decided that Mongo Braima should be paid a visit next morning.

The weather now took a hand. The night began hot and sultry, and as the ships were tied up alongside the bush, conditions on board became unbearable. With not a breath of wind to stir the air, it was impossible to sleep below decks, and on the open deck things were no better. Swarms of vicious fever-bearing mosquitoes attacked any exposed flesh, and wild animals lurking in the nearby bush howled and roared like demented fiends. Then, just before midnight, a tornado struck.

The West African tornado lacks the destructive force of the tornadoes of the American plains, but is none the less an unpleasant experience. It begins similarly as a dark cloud, which thickens as it approaches, and there is a noticeable drop in temperature. Then without warning a violent wind springs up, often reaching storm force and usually blowing from the east. The wind is accompanied by torrential rain, thunder, and spectacular displays of forked lightning.

At dawn on the 18th it was still raining heavily, but the wind had dropped. The storm had left *Snapper* high and dry on the river bank, but she was in no danger, while *Thistle* was battered, but still afloat. With full daylight the rain eased slightly, the boats were brought alongside again, and Chisholm boarded with his men. They landed on the same stretch of beach, and marched inland to search for Chief Mongo Braima. After the heavy rains of the night the going was hard, and with no guide to lead the way they were soon lost in the thick jungle. Chisholm persisted, and after three hours spent slogging through ankle-deep mud, and following paths that led nowhere, they finally emerged into a wide clearing containing a collection of huts that Mongo Braima

73

called his town. As if to celebrate their discovery, the rains stopped and the sun came out again.

Taking advantage of the element of surprise, Captain Chisholm ordered his men to attack the town as soon as they broke free of the jungle. There was sporadic resistance at first, but in the face of heavy and determined fire from the British troops, Mongo Braima's men soon faded into the bush. A search of the buildings showed that the town was deserted, and Chisholm ordered all the buildings, including a warehouse packed with merchandise belonging to Thomas Curtis, to be put to the torch. When the town was well alight, the party returned to the ships empty handed.

The two combined operations carried out ashore had failed to bring about the release of the *Thistle*'s missing men, but although the landing party had been up against vastly superior forces fighting on their own ground – Chisholm estimated his men were outnumbered by twenty to one – the cost to the expedition had not been great. One corporal of marines had died of heat exhaustion, and one marine and two soldiers of the 2nd West India Regiment had been wounded. It was a small price to pay for two operations carried out under extremely difficult conditions.

With *Snapper* aground on the mud, the immediate task when Chisholm returned was to refloat her. Hawsers were passed to the boats, a stream anchor carried out into the river and laid. When the tide was on the flood, the boats took the strain, the anchor cable was taken to the windlass, and by early afternoon *Snapper* was afloat and none the worse for grounding. Unfortunately, as she was moving downstream towed by the boats, she fouled *Thistle*'s hawsers, causing the other brig to run aground.

Lieutenant Hagan attempted to get *Thistle* off the mud with a stream anchor, but the tide was already falling, and all his efforts failed. In the end, he was forced to accept the unpleasant fact that his ship would not move until the next high water, then twelve hours away. As a precaution against attack during the night, Leeke landed a party of troops, who took up a defensive position on shore.

But Lady Luck had not entirely deserted the expedition. Early that evening Leeke had the satisfaction of seeing two of *Thistle*'s missing seamen return in a canoe. Their release had been obtained by one of Mongo Braima's neighbours, King Yando Coney, who the returning men said was anxious for the safety of his own town. The punitive action undertaken by Chisholm and his landing party had not been in vain.

During the night there was more good news, when the trader Wilson arrived on board *Thistle*. He reported that, through the intervention of himself and John Ormond, Curtis had freed the remaining four prisoners. A boat with a party of marines was immediately sent up river with Wilson, and returned with the four seamen just before midnight. As soon as they were aboard, the tide being right, an attempt was made to heave *Thistle* off the mud. This was again unsuccessful, and the brig spent the rest of the night high and dry, being finally refloated at 11.30 next morning. Both ships then crossed the bar to rejoin *Myrmidon* and *Morgiana*, and the squadron set sail for Freetown, arriving there on 23 May.

Captain James Chisholm summed up the operation in his report to the governor, Lieutenant-Colonel Macarthy, written on passage to Freetown:

> The principal object of the expedition being accomplished, by the restoration of these men to the service of their country, and the punishment of the savages who so barbarously put their comrades to death after their surrender, the squadron is to return to Sierra Leone without delay.
>
> I feel great pleasure in reporting to you that the behaviour of the troops has been highly satisfactory to me. The conquest of a large district of woody country, defended by an armed body of men, which the neighbouring inhabitants say exceeded 3,500, and the destruction of several towns, with an inconsiderable loss on our side is to be ascribed to the resolute conduct of the conjoined forces in the attack on Curtis Town.
>
> I cannot close this report without expressing my sense of the advantages, which the expedition received from the zeal and experience of Captain Leeke. His arrangements for the landing of the troops and the firing from the ships of war under his immediate directions produced the effect he anticipated... .

Chapter Seven

The Brief Alliance

Lieutenant James Still

Sacred to the Memory of Lieutenant James Still R.N. who in the 22nd year of his age, fell a victim to the ravages of Yellow Fever, on board His Majesty's Ship, The Pheasant, while stationed off Sierra Leone, on the 12th October 1821. For four successive years he had been employed in the fatal service of enforcing obedience to the sacred Law, which to the honour of his Country and in the spirit of Christian Love, forbade the traffic in human blood.

Memorial at St. Mary of the Virgin Church, Nottingham

Encouraged by the success of the Rio Pongas expedition, Sir George Collier ordered the captains of the African Squadron to press home the advantage by patrolling closer inshore and, wherever possible, to penetrate deep into every estuary likely to be harbouring slavers. This was a lot to ask of men who were more at home in the North Sea and English Channel, few of whom had any local knowledge, and whose charts showed only the vaguest detail of inshore waters. Crossing the bar at the entrance of a West African river was a lottery with the odds heavily loaded against the ship, and every incursion inland was fraught with too many dangers to contemplate. However, the fight went on, and by the end of 1820, certainly as far as British slavers were concerned, this aggressive policy was paying dividends. Very few British ships were now prepared to run the gauntlet of the African Squadron while carrying slaves, and their owners were forced to look around for other more legitimate cargoes. The Industrial Revolution was gathering pace at home, and one of the raw materials most in demand was palm oil, the basic ingredient of soap, candles, medicines and lubricants. The oil palm grew in profusion in the steamy heat of the Bight of Biafra, the oil from its seeds selling at £14 a ton on the Calabar River and fetching double that price in Europe. The profit to be made on shipping barrels of the golden oil or bags of palm kernels easily matched that to be made by carrying human cargoes, and this without any of the dangers and disadvantages of the slave trade. For the British shipowner the infamous Slave Rivers became the equally lucrative Oil Rivers.

The United States of America, in line with Britain, had outlawed the slave trade in 1807, a move which threatened the survival of the economy of the Southern States, which was heavily dependent on a steady supply of slaves. There were many in the North who strongly disagreed with the practices of the plantation owners in the South, but the time had not yet arrived when the two sides would be prepared to go to war to defend their differing points of view. In consequence, the American slaving fleet, second only in size to that of Britain, continued to sail, assisted by Spanish and Portuguese ships, to service the labour demands of the southern plantations.

An anti-slavery bill passed by the US Congress gave President James Monroe the authority to send ships of the US Navy into West African waters to seize any American ships engaged in carrying slaves. The first ship appointed to this task was the 539-ton frigate *Cyane*, ironically, a British ship captured from the Royal Navy in the war of 1812-14. Commanded by Captain Edward Trenchard, the USS *Cyane* was armed with four 12-pounders, twenty 32-pounder carronades and eight 18-pounder carronades.

The *Cyane* sailed in February 1820, escorting the brig *Elizabeth*, chartered by the American Colonization Society to carry eighty-six freed slaves back to West Africa where, taking another leaf out of the British book, the Americans intended to set up a colony on Sherbro Island, some 60 miles south of Freetown. Trenchard's first lieutenant in the *Cyane* was Lieutenant Matthew C. Perry who, in later years, as Admiral Perry, would be mainly responsible for opening up Japan to the rest of the world.

On the long passage across the Atlantic, twenty-five of the *Elizabeth*'s passengers died of fever, and those who survived the voyage were landed in Freetown. Later, they were moved south to the Grain Coast, the new location for the American colony. Their reception on arrival was hostile, for the area was the base for a number of slave traders who had no wish to see their businesses threatened. Fighting broke out between the two factions, but with the help of the guns of the *Cyane* the new country of Liberia came into being, its capital being named Monrovia in honour of President Monroe, the man behind its birth.

Having discharged his duty to the freed slaves, Captain Trenchard took the *Cyane* back to the north, looking for illicit slavers. He did not have to look far. On 10 April, only 70 miles from Monrovia, he intercepted six ships in the Gallinas River all engaged in loading slaves. Trenchard was convinced that these ships were American owned and manned, but they all had Spanish names and were sailing under the Spanish flag. Their papers, issued in Havana, appeared to be genuine, so Trenchard had no legal grounds for detaining them. The American captain's introduction to the devious ways of the West African slave traders had come early.

In September of that year, *Cyane* was joined by the 24-gun frigate *John Adams*, commanded by Captain H.S. Wadsworth, and the brig *Hornet*, Captain Robert F. Stockton. Later, the squadron was augmented by the arrival of the schooners *Alligator* and *Shark*, two fast Baltimore-built clippers, each mounting twelve guns, and ideally suited for the inshore work required to flush out the slavers. In October, having shown the way for the US Navy's African Squadron, *Cyane* left the coast to return home.

On 22 October, the *John Adams* arrived off the Rio Pongas looking for slavers, where she met up with HMS *Snapper*, then keeping watch at the entrance to the river. *Snapper*'s commander, Lieutenant Nash, was aware that several ships were up river loading slaves, but he did not have enough men or boats to mount a cutting-out operation. The American frigate, on the other hand, had a surplus of men and a large double-banked pulling barge, and when Captain Wadsworth suggested a combined operation, Nash readily agreed. There followed a rare example of cooperation between the two navies, neither of which had shown any trust in the other since the war of 1812.

Next morning, the *John Adams*'s barge was put over the side and, manned by an Anglo-American force led by Wadsworth and Nash, crossed the bar and rowed up river to seek out the slavers. After a hot, exhausting pull in temperatures up to 120° F, they eventually came on several schooners hiding in a creek awaiting their cargoes of slaves. The ships were boarded, but although they were plainly Americans equipped for slaving, they flew the Spanish flag, and Wadsworth was unable to take action against them. Nash urged him to turn a Nelsonian eye to the flags, but the American captain was adamant, and the barge returned down river empty handed.

This failed expedition had dire results for the *John Adams*. She continued to patrol off the river entrance, but within a few days ten of her crew were down with malaria, probably as a result of mosquito bites received while they were up river with the barge. By the middle of November three of these men had died. Then on the 21st of the month, having like the *Cyane* before her achieved nothing worthy of note, the *John Adams* was recalled for duty in the Caribbean. That left the US African Squadron with only a brig and two schooners, and a dwindling enthusiasm for the job in hand. Soon they too were withdrawn, and more than twenty years would elapse before the US Navy again played any significant part in the suppression of the slave trade.

On the West African coast the harmattan blows from December to February, in what is aptly called the dry season. This hot wind is laden with the dust of the Sahara, which shrouds the coast in a thick haze that persists throughout the day. The new year of 1821 was no exception, the poor visibility adding yet another burden to the lot of the Royal Navy's ships. Inshore patrolling was an extremely hazardous operation, and boat work in the rivers almost impossible. It was not until the March rains cleared the air that Sir George Collier's ships were again able to come to grips with their enemy.

Early in March the brig *Tartar*, with Sir George on board, in company with Lieutenant Hagan's *Thistle*, was off the entrance to the River Bonny following up intelligence received of slave traders, probably Spaniards, at work in the river. The Bonny area was home to the people of the Ibo and Fulani tribes, much sought after by the slavers for their superior physique and intelligence. The river, which flows into the Bight of Biafra, is deep and wide, navigable many miles inland, but if the slavers were to be caught red-handed, the element of surprise was essential. Conscious that *Tartar*'s tall masts would be visible above the tops of the trees, Commodore Collier anchored the brig well off the river and sent the smaller *Thistle* in under Spanish colours.

Not having been into the Bonny River before, Lieutenant Hagan approached the entrance with caution, but once over the bar he had no difficulty in moving up river. *Thistle* had not progressed more than a few miles, and was still within sight of *Tartar*, when she saw a schooner anchored close in to the bank. Hagan examined her through the glass and concluded that she was almost certainly a slaver. As previously arranged with Commodore Collier, he then signalled *Tartar*, asking her to send in her boats to board the stranger.

As Hagan moved closer to the schooner, a large canoe manned by a dozen paddlers shot out from the near bank and came alongside *Thistle*. In the canoe was a local pilot who, obviously mistaking the British ship for a Spanish slaver, offered to guide Hagan to a safe anchorage where slaves were available. Hagan's answer was to commandeer the canoe and man it with a party of thirty armed men led by Midshipman Charles Lyons. The midshipman's orders were to board and search the schooner, using whatever force was necessary.

When Lyons got alongside the schooner, her crew were on deck and manning their guns but, by keeping his men out of sight in the bottom of the canoe until the last minute, he gained the element of surprise. He led his men in boarding the schooner, and he and two others were slightly wounded in the fight that followed. The resistance was fierce but short-lived, and the ship – she was the Spanish-flag *Anna Maria* of 172 tons, registered in Havana, and under the command of Captain Mateo Sánchez – was soon in British hands. Unfortunately, in the heat of the hand-to-hand battle, fifty female slaves, who were on deck, became so terrified that they threw themselves over the side. There were sharks in the water, and none of the women survived to reach the shore.

Incredibly for such a tiny vessel, the *Anna Maria* had been carrying 500 slaves. Sir George Collier described the conditions they were living under: 'They were clinging to the gratings to inhale a mouthful of fresh air, and fighting with each other for a taste of water, showing their parched tongues and pointing to their reduced stomachs, as if overcome by famine for, although the living cargo had only been completed the day before, yet many who had been longer in the boats were reduced to such a state as skeletons that I was obliged to order 12 to be immediately placed under the care of the surgeon...' The 450 slaves remaining on board were found to be shackled together in pairs; some of them, troublemakers, perhaps, were also tied up with ropes, 'their arms so lacerated that the flesh was completely eaten through...'

The *Anna Maria*, with a prize crew on board, was sent to Freetown, where her slaves were set free. On his return to Freetown, Commodore Collier learned that his prize had been in front of the court before, having been arrested by HMS *Myrmidon*. Unfortunately, the *Anna Maria* had no slaves on board on that occasion, and the court was forced to release her. She had subsequently, so it was revealed, taken on a full cargo of slaves in the River Gallinas and, eluding the British patrols, had delivered them to Havana, no doubt reaping a fat profit for Captain Sánchez and her owners. Now, caught red-handed, the Spanish ship had reached the end of her days in the infamous trade. On 16 June, she was condemned by the Prize Court, and broken up.

As the year progressed, *Tartar* and *Thistle* having returned to Freetown, the Bonny River continued to attract French and Spanish slavers like bees to honey. News of the activity on the river reached Commodore Collier, but his resources were severely limited. The African Squadron, in attempting to patrol the 3,500 miles of coast from Cape Verde to the Gabon, was stretched beyond all sensible limits. Eventually Collier was able to send just one ship to the Bonny River. She was Captain Henry Leeke's 20-gun frigate *Myrmidon*.

Leeke arrived off the entrance to the Bonny River on 10 August, having information that a number of ships were up river loading slaves. With only the one ship at his disposal, and with no pilot available, he decided to anchor off rather than risk taking

Myrmidon into the river. As so often was the case on this coast, the real work had to be done by the ship's boats, and for this the element of surprise was essential. If the boats entered the river by the main channel, they would be seen by the slavers long before they drew near. Fortunately, Captain Leeke knew of a narrow boat channel used by local fisherman which meandered through little known backwaters, and should allow the boats to arrive off Bonny Town unseen.

In the grey light of early dawn next morning *Myrmidon*'s boats were lowered to the water, and the armed men for the expedition boarded. The oars were manned, and wallowing awkwardly in the heavy groundswell, the boats struck out for the shore. Leading in the gig was Lieutenant Bingham, who had command of the expedition. His orders from Leeke were quite specific: to explore the river as far as Bonny Town, and above if deemed necessary, and to board and arrest any ships found taking on slaves or suspected to be equipped for carrying slaves. Any French ships met with, even if engaged in slaving, were to be left alone. Although France had followed the British lead and abolished the slave trade in 1815, French slavers were still very active on the West African coast; but as a result of an Admiralty Court judgement, the Royal Navy was forbidden to interfere with them. This bizarre judgement was given following the boarding of the French slaver *Louis* off Liberia in 1817 by HMS *Princess Charlotte*. The master of the *Louis*, Captain Jean Forest, appealed to the Admiralty Court in London, and the judge, Sir William Scott, decided in his favour. Scott declared, 'I can find no authority which gives us the right of interruption to the navigation of states in amity upon the high seas.' He added, 'To procure an eminent good by means that are unlawful is not consonant with private morality.' The judgement was final, thus giving all French slavers immunity from interference by the Royal Navy.

Once across the bar, Bingham made for the gap in the mangrove-fronted shore that marked the entrance to the narrow boat channel known by the locals as the Anthony River. The oarsmen bent their backs to counteract the pull of a cross current, and with the gig leading, the boats shot through the gap into the placid waters of the creek. The banks were shrouded in an early morning mist, through which came a muted chorus of barks and growls from the beasts of the forest disturbed by the slap of oars on water. In the half-light of dawn men accustomed to facing dangerous enemies on sea and on land without flinching looked around nervously and gripped their weapons tighter. For Lieutenant Bingham, who carried the weight of command, this was truly a voyage into the unknown. Other than that the channel would eventually lead them to Bonny, he had no idea of what lay ahead.

There was something ghostly, almost evil, about this strange creek that lent strength to the oarsmen's arms, and as the sun lifted above the horizon to dispel the mists of the night, the boats suddenly burst out into open water, and they were within sight of Bonny Town. At anchor off the untidy cluster of huts scattered amongst the mangroves that masqueraded as a town were six ships.

As the boats drew near, Bingham saw that the ships were all flying the French flag, and they were quite obviously taking on slaves. This was clearly in breach of the French abolition act, but he had explicit orders not to interfere with them. He did, however, lay the gig alongside one of them, and boarded alone. He was courteously received by the French captain, who volunteered the information that two Spanish vessels with slaves on board were further up river.

Bingham now decided to split his force, continuing up river with the gig and the pinnace, and leaving the other boats at Bonny. Rounding the first bend, he came upon a brig and a schooner anchored in midstream; neither had their colours flying, but he suspected they must be the Spanish slavers. He approached cautiously, firing a few musket shots in the air to announce his presence, but there was no response from the deck of either ship.

When the boats were within 25 yards of the brig, Bingham shouted a challenge. This produced an immediate reaction. The Spaniards, who had been crouching behind their bulwarks, opened the gun ports and swept the British boats with a hail of musket fire and grape shot.

The gig was hardest hit, the two officers in the boat, Lieutenant Bingham and Midshipman Deschamps both being severely injured. Two seamen were also wounded. Bingham, hit in the chest by grapeshot, appeared to be mortally wounded, and

Deschamps, although bleeding profusely from a head wound, took command. On his orders, the boats pulled away from the Spaniard and retired down river, still under heavy fire.

When informed of the failure of the boats to board the Spaniards, Captain Leeke sent in more men with orders to make another attempt. By the time the boats arrived up river, however, the Spanish sailors had built barricades around their bulwarks, and it would clearly be impossible to board the ships without suffering heavy casualties. Once more the British boats were forced to retreat down river.

With his boats back alongside and the wounded on board, Leeke came to the conclusion that the only way he would be able to seize the Spanish slavers was by taking the *Myrmidon* into the river. As there was no pilot available, this was a risky venture, and could not be hurried. Firstly, he had to find his way across the treacherous sandbanks that barred the way into the Bonny River, and this could only be done by resorting to basic seamanship. Boats were sent in to take soundings, and after days of painstaking work a channel deep enough for *Myrmidon* was found and buoyed.

Rather than risk running his ship aground, Captain Leeke decided to wait for the ideal weather and tidal conditions. These did not occur until three weeks later, leaving *Myrmidon* swinging idle at her anchor and Leeke consumed with frustration. At last, on 31 August, conditions were right, and soon after dawn *Myrmidon*'s draught was lightened considerably by putting all men not required in handling the ship into the boats. Then, with leadsmen in the chains continuously sounding the bottom, the sloop inched her way across the bar. The delicate operation took all day, and the sun was setting by the time *Myrmidon* anchored in the river.

Next morning, Leeke weighed anchor and moved cautiously up river. When *Myrmidon* was abreast of Bonny Town, a canoe came alongside bearing a letter from the captains of the Spanish slavers. It seems that the mere sight of *Myrmidon*'s tall masts, visible over the tops of the trees, had been enough to send the Spaniards into a blind panic. Both crews had abandoned their ships and had taken refuge ashore. In the letter, the captains pleaded guilty to firing on Bingham's boats and begged Leeke not to charge them with an act of piracy. In return, they offered their ships as prizes.

When the two abandoned Spanish ships were boarded, it was found that the brig had 154 slaves chained up in her hold and the schooner another 139. Prize crews were put on board to take the captured ships down river and on to Freetown where they were disposed of, and the slaves freed. Meanwhile, Leeke sent men ashore to round up the Spanish crews. Both captains later appeared before the court in Freetown charged with firing on boats of the Royal Navy engaged on their lawful business. Lieutenant Bingham had recovered from his wounds, and the captains were convicted of piracy rather than murder, although the penalty, death by hanging, was the same.

In April 1822 *Myrmidon* returned to the Bonny River in company with the brig *Iphigenia*. Captain Henry Leeke was still in command of *Myrmidon*, while the new commodore of the African Squadron, Sir Robert Mends, flew his flag in *Iphigenia*. Mends was an officer of great experience, having fought in many campaigns, losing an arm in the American War of Independence when a midshipman aged only thirteen. His new assignment would require all his expertise and experience. Despite the efforts of the Squadron, slave trading in the Bonny River and its near neighbour the Calabar had continued to flourish, no fewer than thirty-five cargoes sailing for the Americas from the two rivers in the previous four months. The French, it was reported, were carrying the bulk of the trade.

Acting on information that a number of ships had recently arrived in the river to take on slaves, *Iphigenia* and *Myrmidon* anchored off the entrance to the Bonny late in the afternoon of Sunday 14 April. Having been well briefed by Captain Leeke on the resistance met with when the *Myrmidon*'s boats last entered the river, Commodore Mends decided that a strong show of force was called for, but that at the same time the element of surprise must be preserved.

At 4 o'clock next morning, while it was still dark, with the minimum of noise and showing no lights, both ships lowered their boats to the water and embarked the boarding parties. The small flotilla of boats, three from each ship, carried a total of 150 armed men, the operation being under the command of Lieutenant William St. John Mildmay, *Iphigenia*'s first lieutenant.

Some of the boats had a light gun mounted in the bows, but the expedition would have to rely chiefly on muskets and swords should it come to a fight. The question of whether the Navy was justified in interfering with French slavers had still not been resolved, and Mildmay was under orders from Mends not to attempt to board any French ships found in the river.

The morning was fine, but there was a fresh breeze blowing off the land, and the tide being on the ebb, the crowded boats made slow progress towards the shore. Dawn was breaking as they crossed the bar, and by the time they entered the river the sun was climbing over the horizon. Mildmay, leading in *Iphigenia*'s pinnace, steadied his long glass on the mast, and focused on a cluster of ships which appeared to be at anchor 4 miles or so up river. Soon, he was able to identify them as a brigantine, four brigs, and two schooners, all of indeterminate nationality, but assumed by Mildmay to be either French or Spanish. He ordered the boats to hoist their colours.

As the boats drew nearer to the anchorage, the two schooners, which were anchored in mid-stream and facing up river into the ebb tide, began to swing across the river. To Lieutenant Mildmay this indicated that the schooners probably had springs on their cables, a common practice when anchored in a river, especially in naval ships. A hawser was made fast to the anchor cable low down on the water, and led aft outside the ship to be brought back aboard at the stern to the capstan. This acted as a lever, and when the weight was taken on the hawser, the ship swung across the tide to present her broadside. Any doubts Mildmay might have had as to the purpose of this little gathering in the Bonny River were quickly dispelled. These were slavers, and they meant to fight.

The schooners, as Mildmay was later to learn, were both Spanish-flag, the 306-ton *Yeatam*, armed with eight long 18-pounders and two long 9-pounders, and the smaller 180-ton *Vecua*, mounting eight long 18-pounders and one long 9-pounder. As soon as the British boats came within range, both schooners opened fire with a full broadside of canister and grapeshot, backed up by musket fire. The musket balls fell short, for the range was too great, but the canister and grapeshot turned the water around the boats into a boiling maelstrom of falling shot.

1. Anti-slavery campaigner William Wilberforce MP
(Africa Christian Action)

2. Slaves freed by British military expedition

(Africa Christian Action)

3. Slave caravan on the long march to the coast   *(Africa Christian Action)*

4. Slave market i
Zanzibar
*(Africa Christian
Action)*

5. Arab slave caravan resting   *(Africa Christian Action)*

6. Arab slave caravan
reaches coast
(Africa Christian Action)

7. Royal Navy pinnace puts shots across bows of suspect slaver   *(Africa Christian Action)*

8. Sick slaves being thrown overboard from Liverpool slaver *Zong*   *(Musée de la Marine)*

9. Captain John Newton
(Christian Links)

10. Surgeon William
Loney RN
(P. Davis)

11. Memorial to Captain Bird Allen RN in St. Mary's Church, Tenby   *(Author)*

12. Details of memorial in St. Mary's Church, Tenby   *(Author)*

SACRED TO THE MEMORY

OF

CAPTAIN **BIRD ALLEN R.N.**

WHO IN THE 38TH YEAR OF HIS AGE

DIED AT FERNANDO PO THE 25TH OF OCTR 1841.

WHILE IN COMMAND OF H.M.S. SOUDAN.

ON AN EXPEDITION INTO THE INTERIOR OF

AFRICA,

TO PROMOTE THE INTRODUCTION OF CHRISTIANITY AND CIVILIZAT

O THAT COUNTRY. HIS FRIENDS HAVE ERECTED THIS TABLET

ORD THEIR STRONG SENSE OF HIS CHRISTIAN EXCELLENCE AN

NAL TALENTS, AND TO TESTIFY THEIR DEEP REGRET FOR HIS L

AND THAT OF HIS BRAVE COMPANIONS WHO WITH HIM

FELL VICTIMS TO THE CLIMATE OF THE RIVER NIGER.

MARK THE PERFECT MAN, AND BEHOLD THE UPRIGHT:

FOR THE END OF THAT MAN IS PEACE.   PSALM. 57. V 37.

13. Cape Coast Castle

(*Africa Christian Action*)

14. St. Thomas (São Tome) Island. The slaves' last glimpse of Africa   (*Captain Peter Smimov*)

15. U.S. slaver *Wanderer*   *(US Dept of the Navy)*

16. HMS *Black Joke* in pursuit of the Spanish slaver *El Almirante*   *(Africa Christian Action)*

Two of the brigs and the brigantine also opened fire to add to the barrage. Mildmay returned the fire with his own guns, but to little effect. It was obvious to him that the only chance of success lay in boarding and taking the ships before their combined firepower blew his boats out of the water. He called on his oarsmen to row for their lives.

Picking up speed as the beat of their oars increased, the boats came through the fire storm unscathed, and within twenty minutes the first was alongside and boarding the *Yeatam*. In the fierce fight that followed, sixteen of the schooner's crew were killed, and the rest threw down their arms. Meanwhile, the crew of the other schooner, the *Vecua*, had abandoned their ship and fled ashore, but not before setting a scuttling charge in her magazine. Luckily for Mildmay's boarding party, and for the 300 slaves found chained below in the schooner's hold, the charge was discovered and its fuse extinguished before the ship blew up.

It transpired that the other ships which had fired on the boats were flying the French flag, and as far as Lieutenant Mildmay was concerned, by firing on him they had committed an act of piracy, which justified their arrest. All three were boarded and taken after a fight. They were the 240-ton brig *Vigilante*, manned by a crew of thirty men and mounting four 12-pounder carronades; the brig *La Petite Betsey* of 184 tons, with a crew of twenty-five and carrying four 9-pounder carronades; and the 100-ton brigantine *L'Ursule*, also mounting four 9-pounder carronades, and manned by twenty-five men.

In what had been a prolonged battle against very strong French and Spanish opposition, the British boarding parties lost two men killed, while seven others were wounded. The reward for this brave action was the liberation of 1,876 slaves.

Sir Robert Mends escorted all five slavers to Freetown to be dealt with by the court. Unfortunately, during the passage the *Yeatam* became detached from the others, and capsized when she was hit by a tornado, with the loss of all 400 slaves and fifteen of her prize crew of twenty-three. Two hundred other slaves sickened and died in the other ships. However, with regard to the French slavers taken, the efforts of Lieutenant William St. John Mildmay and his brave men appear to have been in vain. The following appeared in the *Times* of 26 August 1822:

The two French vessels *Vigilante* and *L'Ursule*, which were captured by the boats of His Majesty's ships *Iphigenia*, Sir Robert Mends, and *Myrmidon*, Captain Leeke, after such a severe contest, in the River Bonny, have been released, and sailed yesterday for Cherbourg. The one which put into Plymouth (*La Petite Betsey*) is also ordered to be sent to the same port. It appears to us unaccountable that these vessels should be restored, after having been captured five degrees Northward of the Line, with several hundred slaves actually on board, and so trading (as we have always understood) contrary to express treaties. Now, our Government will have to pay to the captors about £10 a head bounty money for each slave, and, most probably, be obliged to give the owners of the vessels as much money for their cargoes of human flesh, and souls of men, as they would have realised for them in the West Indies, had the vessels reached those islands (which was physically impossible) with every individual slave on board. The breach of faith in due observance of the slave abolition treaties (as they are called), by France, Spain and Portugal, as well as the abuses so early introduced, and so fatally generated in the Courts of the Mixed Commission at Sierra Leone, were fully exposed by the despatches of Sir George Collier, laid before Parliament in the last session, which excited the most lively and philanthrophic feeling among all ranks of the legislature, and produced the memorable decision and address to the King on the 28th of June last, which speaks so clearly and manfully, and so firmly, the wishes and expectations of the country upon the slave cause.

Chapter Eight

The Two Rivers

Lieutenant Robert Card

Sacred to the memory of Robert Card, late in His Majesty's Navy, and of this town. Zealous and brave in discharging his duty to his King and Country, after constant Employment during the war from his earliest years he was appointed First Lieutenant of the Redwing, stationed to promote the abolition of the slave trade and died of malignant fever off Whydah on the coast of Guinea the 16th March 1826 aged 32 years. His amiable qualities endeared him to all his associates, who with his beloved relations will mourn their loss.

Memorial at St. Mary's Church, Wareham, Dorset

At daylight on 23 October 1822 the 20-gun sloop HMS *Cyrene* was approaching the coast in the vicinity of the Gallinas River. Commanded by Captain Percy Grace, the sloop had left Freetown twenty-four hours earlier with orders from Sir Robert Mends to investigate reports of slaving activity on the Gallinas.

For many years after being discovered by the Portuguese in the 17th century, the Gallinas had been a mecca for slave traders, but the trade had fallen off after the arrival of the African Squadron. However, recent intelligence reaching Freetown reported that the local ruler, King Siaca, had gone into the business of selling his own people into slavery on a large scale. His barracoons were said to be full to overflowing.

The land in the vicinity of the Gallinas River is low and comparatively featureless, the few prominent landmarks being difficult to identify. As a precaution, Captain Grace had shortened sail during the night, not increasing speed until first light. Then, with lookouts posted at the masthead, the *Cyrene* coasted in, running before a light westerly breeze. The entrance to the Gallinas River is not easy to identify from seawards, being obscured by a sand barrier created by the outflow of the Gallinas and its neighbouring river the Sulima. Grace was looking for the hills at the back of Cape Mount, 20 miles south-east of the entrance and the only prominent landmark in the vicinity of the river.

Even with the wind abaft the beam, *Cyrene* was making only a shade over 3 knots, and the sun was overhead before she ran into soundings. Thereafter, with a leadsman in the chains and calling out the decreasing depths, she moved in cautiously. Grace was very much relieved when, shortly after noon, he was able to identify the prominent wooded hills behind Cape Mount, and then the cape itself. The visibility was excellent, Cape Mount in Grace's estimation being then over 30 miles off. He adjusted his course and continued to close the coast.

Half an hour later a hail from the masthead reported a sail on *Cyrene*'s lee bow. Grace raised his glass and swept the horizon, focusing on two specks of white visible to port. Two ships under sail, and probably schooners, Grace decided. They could be slavers just out of the Gallinas River. He altered course to intercept. The wind was still very light, a cast of the log showing that *Cyrene* was now making less than 3 knots. The chase promised to be a long one.

By late afternoon the breeze had at last freshened and *Cyrene* was slowly gaining on her quarry, the nearer schooner being some 3 miles ahead. Then, shortly before sunset the schooners separated, the larger vessel continuing to the south-east, while the smaller one tacked to the north. Grace opted to hold his course, hoping to catch up with the nearer, and larger, schooner.

Cyrene, with all possible sail set, had increased her speed to 4 knots, but the schooner held her own for more than an hour. Finally, at 7 o'clock, with darkness fast closing in, *Cyrene* was almost within musket range of the schooner, and Grace ordered his marines to open fire on her.

The distance was still too great for the musket balls to do any damage, but the mere crackle of gunfire was enough to make someone aboard the schooner have second thoughts about running away. She lowered her sails and waited for *Cyrene*'s boarding party.

Grace sent a lieutenant and nine men to take possession of the ship, the crew of which surrendered without resistance. The boarding party reported back to Grace that she was the 144-ton Dutch schooner *Aurora*, armed with four small calibre guns, and originally from St. Thomas Island. She had no slaves on board, but she was obviously fully equipped to carry them. When questioned, her crew had a strange tale to tell.

The *Aurora*, in company with the other schooner, the 95-ton French-flag *Hypolite*, had been marking time on the coast for two months waiting for a cargo of slaves promised by King Siaca. The negotiations had dragged on, and the master of the *Aurora*, Benjamin Liebray, along with Louis Gallon, master of the *Hypolite* and a number of other crew members from both ships, were still ashore when the British sloop appeared on the scene.

Cyrene was hove to for an hour while securing the *Aurora*, by which time it was dark, and the *Hypolite* was out of sight, but she had been observed to be running to the south-west before darkness fell. Grace went after her, and by 10 o'clock, in the light of the moon, the *Hypolite* was visible on *Cyrene*'s lee bow at about 7 miles. When she caught sight of the British ship, the Frenchman immediately went about and attempted to get away to the north again. *Cyrene* followed in her wake, and by midnight had closed the gap to 2 miles. By 1 o'clock on the morning of the 24th the *Cyrene* was within gunshot range, and Grace fired a shot across the fleeing schooner's bows. The warning shot was enough to persuade the *Hypolite*'s crew that resistance was futile. They furled their sails and hove to. Grace sent away a boat with a midshipman and five armed men, who took possession of the schooner without a struggle.

At noon on the 24th *Cyrene*, with her two prizes, was about 33 miles to the north-west of Cape Mount. At 7.30 that evening the three ships anchored in 11 fathoms, 4 miles off the entrance to the River Gallinas. Next morning, before it was fully light, Grace sent away his pinnace, cutter and one of the gigs, carrying a heavily armed force under the command of Lieutenant George Courtney. With Courtney were Lieutenant George Pigot, William

Hunter, 2nd Master, and Midshipmen Henry Winsor and Malcolm M'Neale. Lieutenant Courtney's orders were to find King Siaca and, if possible, persuade him to release the slaves he was holding. Failing that, Courtney was to use whatever force was necessary to free the slaves. Anticipating casualties, Grace sent *Cyrene*'s surgeon, James Boyle, with the party.

The tide was ebbing strongly, and with a 1 knot current running to the west the boats made slow progress towards the shore. As they battled through a tremendous surf breaking on the bar, the cutter broached to and was swamped. Fortunately, the boat did not sink, but all the loose gear on board and some of her arms and ammunition were lost in the surf. This was a poor beginning for what promised to be a hazardous operation – and there was worse to come.

Where the Gallinas River flows into the sea the distance from bank to bank is only 200 yards, and as the *Cyrene*'s boats entered the river they came under sustained musket fire from both sides. Courtney's men returned the fire as best they could, but as the effective range of a musket was only 100 yards at the most, neither side inflicted any damage or casualties on the other. However, the fact that their arrival in the river had been greeted in such a hostile manner boded ill for the British landing parties.

Pulling hard against the ebbing tide, the boats pushed on up stream, and when they were about a mile inland they came within sight of a cluster of islands. Courtney headed for the largest island, on which were a number of buildings. This was Factory Island, on which the slave traders, believed to be Spanish, had their warehouses and slave barracoons. Unknown to Courtney, the island was defended by two long 18-pounders and an 8-inch mortar, all of which opened fire when the boats drew near.

Courtney's flotilla was now in a very exposed position, and the river at this point had many unseen shallow stretches, which called for painstaking navigation. Raked by grapeshot and musket fire, and stemming a strong tide, it was inevitable that the heavily laden craft grounded frequently on the sandbanks, leaving them dangerously vulnerable. But there was no going back. Heads down and oars digging deep, *Cyrene*'s seamen urged their boats forward, determined to come to grips with the hidden enemy. Each time a boat grounded, there was no shortage of volunteers to manhandle it back into deep water, and send it on its way.

Once committed, there was no stopping the landing force. Ignoring the hail of musket balls buzzing around their heads like angry bees, the boats went in under the guns of Factory Island, and spilled their landing parties onto the beach. Led by Lieutenant George Courtney, marines and seamen stormed ashore; within minutes they had taken the guns and turned them, first on the fleeing enemy, and then on the banks of the river and a nearby island from which heavy musket fire was being directed at them. They were powerless, however, to intervene when they saw large numbers of slaves being herded into canoes on the other island and being taken up river.

The fight had been short and brutal and, as his men were running short of ammunition, Courtney decided nothing further would be gained by continuing the attack. He had not achieved what he set out to do, in that he had not met King Siaca or freed any slaves, but he felt he could ask no more of his men, one of whom, Alexander Crozier, was very seriously wounded. Three others had slight injuries. Before the landing parties returned to their boats they spiked the enemy's guns and put all warehouses and other buildings in the vicinity to the torch.

With the tide behind them the boats made good speed down river, and although they again came under fire from the shore as they neared the sea, they crossed the bar safely, and by late afternoon they were back alongside *Cyrene*. Once on board, the reckoning was made, and it showed that in this audacious and dangerous operation *Cyrene* had lost only one man – Alexander Crozier having died as he was lifted on board. The slave traders on shore, it was later learned, had suffered heavy casualties, including four Europeans killed, on top of which their base had been destroyed.

A few days later, the raid produced a surprising reaction from King Siaca. He sent a messenger aboard to explain, with a great deal of humility, that he, the King, had been out of the area for some days, and in his absence two European ships' captains, none other than Benjamin Liebray of the *Aurora* and Louis Gallon of the *Hypolite*, had organised the hostile reception Courtney's men received. Siaca claimed that Liebray and Gallon, who with some of their men were on shore collecting slaves, had plied the locals with rum, given them arms, and urged them to kill the visiting Englishmen. By way of compensation, Siaca sent out to the *Cyrene* a party of 180 slaves, which he said the captains had ready to put aboard their own ships. Ironically, the slaves ended up on the *Aurora*, but only for the short passage to Freetown, where they were set free.

With two ships engaged in an illegal trade arrested and 180 slaves freed as a result of their efforts, Captain Grace and the men of the *Cyrene* looked forward to some recompense in the way of prize money. The going rate at the time was £5 for every slave released and landed, and £4 a ton for every slave ship captured. To their great disappointment, the Admiralty in London ruled that as the slaves had not been physically set free by Courtney's men, and the *Aurora* and *Hypolite* had no slaves on board when they were captured, no prize money was payable. Then to rub salt into an already painful wound, both ships were released by the court in Freetown.

Fifteen years after the *Cyrene* raid, despite the continuing efforts of the Royal Navy, it seems that little had changed on the Gallinas. Dr James Hall of the American Colonization Society, on visiting the river in 1837, wrote:

About a mile from the river's mouth we found ourselves among a cluster of islands, on each of which was located the factory of some particular slave merchant. The buildings, generally, consisted of a business room, with warehouse attached, filled with merchandize and provisions, and a barracoon for the slaves; the whole built by by setting rough stakes or small trees into the ground, these being wattled together with withies and covered with thatch. That containing the slaves, being much the strongest and generally surrounded by, or connected with, a yard, in which the slaves were permitted to exercise daily. We think that there were some ten or twelve of these establishments at that time, each containing from 100 to 500 slaves. We believe one contained near 1000, which, it was expected, would be shipped daily. Each barracoon was in charge of from two to four white men, Spanish or Portuguese...We recollect going into one yard where there were some 300 boys, all apparently between ten and fifteen years of age, linked together in squads of twenty or thirty. We never saw a more painfully interesting sight than the long rows of these bright-eyed little fellows, doomed to the horrors of a middle latitude passage, probably in three and a half feet between decks. Another peculiar feature of the place was the collection of long canoes and boats, all kept ready for the dispatch of slaves the moment an opportunity should occur. Probably 1000 slaves could be shipped in four hours, all things favourable....The bar at the river mouth is not unfrequently dangerous, even in the dry season, and in the anxiety to ship the slaves they run great hazards, and many a boat load of poor wretches becomes food for sharks, who always follow such boats and canoes in great numbers...In fact, all connected with this trade is painful and distressing to humanity, and this Gallinas, of all other places on the coast of Africa, with which we have been acquainted, has been the scene of its greatest horrors. What imagination can conceive the thousandth part of the misery that has been endured by human beings of this little cluster of bushy islands? Of the five or ten thousand, who are annually brought to this place, each and every one has to mourn a home made desolate, a family dismembered, the blood of kindred flowing. Of this number, how many sink in these wretched barracoons from distress of mind at their wretched condition, from disease and famine; how many are sacrificed in their hurried shipment by the ravenous sharks; how many sink under the most protracted agonies in that confinement between decks, the air of which is putridity itself...?

Two months after the Gallinas incident, in December 1822, HMS *Cyrene* chased and arrested another French schooner, the *Caroline*. She was found to have only five slaves on board, but Captain Grace considered this reason enough to take the schooner into Freetown. Unfortunately, once again, as in the case of the *Hypolite*, the *Caroline* was released by the court in Freetown. Although France had officially abolished the slave trade in 1818, records show that for twenty years after that the French act of abolition was still without teeth. The French government, always implacably opposed to anything British, refused to allow the Royal Navy to stop and board French ships suspected of slaving. It was conceded that a British man-of-war might approach and hail a French merchant ship to enquire her business. At the discretion of the ship's master, a boat might be sent to inspect the ship's papers, but only to confirm that she had the right to fly the French flag. No search of the ship was permitted. Meanwhile, with the aid of corrupt officials at home and abroad, French ships happily carried on a brisk trade in slaves between West Africa and French plantations in South America and Cuba. There were a few French naval vessels on the coast, but their role was unclear. In June 1822 Sir Charles Macarthy reporting from Freetown on the state of the slave trade in the area, remarked:

> ...the French brig of war *L'Huron*, Commodore Maurice du Plessis, came into this harbour from a cruise to Leewards, I received that officer, who commands the squadron of small vessels of war employed between Senegal and Goree, and on occasional cruises along the coast, with that politeness due to his rank and the friendly relations subsisting between our respective countries, and learned from him with equal regret and surprise that having proceeded as far as Grand Bassa, he fell in with and visited several vessels under the French flag, which he had strong grounds to suspect were employed on the slave trade, but that he did not detain any, as from his instructions he was not authorised to seize any vessel, but such as had slaves on board, that he was particularly anxious to take in water and other articles he required in order to resume his cruise off the Gallinas...

Thanks to the diligence of the African Squadron, after the passing of the Abolition of the Slave Trade Act British ships largely dropped out of the trade, although there were a few diehards who stubbornly refused to change their ways. In March 1824, Parliament, anxious to put an end to British participation in the slave trade once and for all, enacted legislation declaring that any British subject found guilty of trading would be charged with 'felony, piracy and robbery, and should suffer death without the benefit of clergy and loss of land, goods and chattels as pirates, felons and robbers upon the seas ought to suffer.' As far as those few British ships still engaged were concerned, the mere threat posed by this act must have been sufficient to deter them from further involvement in a trade in which they had once excelled. No prosecution was ever brought against a British subject under this act, but there were always others ready to take up the challenge.

The death of Bartholomew Roberts off Cape Lopez in February 1722, and the subsequent public hanging of his crew at Cape Coast Castle, signalled the end of the Golden Age of piracy. For the next ninety years, with the major maritime nations constantly warring, the plundering of the innocent at sea was largely the prerogative of the privateers, operating under letters of marque issued by their respective governments. When, in 1814, the war with America ended, and Britain was once more at peace with France and Spain, thousands of privateers found themselves without employment. Unwilling to turn to legitimate trading some, mainly Spaniards and their colonial cousins from Cuba and Puerto Rico, turned to piracy. However, the pirates of the 19th century were a very different breed, their disgusting conduct often making the likes of the long-gone Edward 'Blackbeard' Teach and 'Calico Jack' Rackam look like gentlemen. Inevitably, the new pirates found their way to the lucrative Gulf of Guinea.

After meandering across West Africa for 2,600 miles, the River Niger finally enters the sea in the notorious Bight of Benin, of which it was said, 'Beware the Bight of Benin, there's one comes out for forty goes in.' This may have been an exaggeration, but certainly no one in the African Squadron would have disputed it, the death rate in the ships in these waters being one in four.

The Benin River is one of the mouths of the Niger, a fever-infested waterway much favoured by Portuguese slavers, who had been actively engaged in exporting slaves from the area to their colonies in South America since the late 1500s. When His Majesty's 20-gun sloop *Esk* arrived off the Benin in March 1826, her commander, Captain William Purchas, found the Portuguese as active as ever.

The approach to the Benin River, like that of so many in West Africa, is a navigator's nightmare. The shore is low-lying, with no conspicuous landmarks, and the entrance to the river is difficult to distinguish from seaward. The bar across the entrance is composed of hard sand, on which a heavy groundswell breaks continuously and sometimes with overwhelming force. For a ship of the *Esk*'s size, passage across the bar was impossible, and even for her boats it would be a very hazardous undertaking. When the sloop arrived off the river on 3 March, Captain Purchas dropped anchor 3 miles outside the bar. It was a safe anchorage, but with only 5 fathoms of water the groundswells were running high. Throughout the rest of that day and the night that followed *Esk* rolled sluggishly in the swell, while Purchas made his preparations.

Next morning, as soon as there was light enough, and before the onshore breeze sprang up, *Esk*'s boats left the ship's side, and battled their way through the surf breaking on the bar. They were three miles up river when they rounded a bend to find a small brigantine anchored off Horsfall Island. It was not difficult to guess what the unidentified vessel was up to, for as soon as the British force was sighted, boats began to leave her side packed with black humanity. She was getting rid of the evidence.

When the brigantine was boarded, she was found to be the 75-ton Brazilian-flag *Netuno*, manned by Portuguese and with a cargo of 150 slaves. By the time the boarding party had secured her, fifty-eight slaves had already reached the shore and disappeared into the jungle. A boat containing another twenty was intercepted before reaching the shore, and seventy-two slaves, including some women and children, were still in the *Netuno*'s hold. The brigantine was arrested and taken out to the anchorage.

Two days later the *Netuno* sailed for Freetown. In command of the Brazilian was Master's Mate Richard Crawford, whose prize crew consisted of 16-year-old Master's Assistant Finch, five seamen, and a boy of 17 named Olivine. Four Portuguese, including *Netuno*'s ex-master, were also on board, along with the ninety-two slaves. The ex-Brazilian's armament consisted of two 6-pounder carronades, a brace of pistols, and six cutlasses, the latter apparently on board to subdue any troublesome slaves. Whether the guns could be handled by the *Netuno*'s small prize crew was in doubt, but as she was sailing in company with the sloop HMS *Redwing*, also bound for Freetown, the occasion seemed unlikely to arise.

The two ships had not long left the coast before it became clear that the *Netuno* was not built for speed. In fact, she was so slow that the exasperated commander of the *Redwing* soon decided to leave her behind.

Two weeks went by with the *Netuno* caught in the Doldrums, making barely 20 miles in a day. At noon on 20 March she had reached a point some 300 miles south of Whydah, with more than 1000 miles to cover before she reached Sierra Leone. Not surprisingly, by this time, with over a hundred people on board, the *Netuno*'s food and water were running low.

At around 3 o'clock that afternoon, a sail was sighted on the larboard quarter, overtaking at a smart pace. As the stranger drew nearer, she was seen to be a square-rigger, and Crawford assumed she must be the *Redwing*, in which case he hoped she would be able to supply him with some fresh water and provisions. He shortened sail to allow the other ship to catch up.

Fifty minutes later the stranger was 2 miles astern, but had not yet hoisted her colours. At 4 o'clock she fired two guns, which Crawford took to be a recognition signal. He hoisted his own colours, took in more sail, and stood towards the other ship, which he was now convinced was – if not the *Redwing* – almost certainly a British man-of-war.

The two ships, both now under shortened sail, slowly converged. Then, when only a mile separated them, Crawford, who had been studying the stranger through his glass, realised that she was not British, and had a hostile look about her. He immediately ordered all sail set, and attempted to get away. It was too late. The other ship broke out the French ensign, opened her gun ports, and put several shots across the *Netuno*'s bow. She then hailed the British prize and ordered her to heave to and wait for a boat to come alongside.

The *Netuno*, whose only armament consisted of two 6-pounder carronades, was hopelessly outgunned, and Crawford had no other option but to lower his sails and wait for the boat. He was suspicious of the nature of the Frenchman's challenge, however, and he gave orders for the 6-pounders to be loaded and made ready. He also sent below for the brace of pistols he had brought with him from the *Esk*.

Crawford's suspicions were confirmed when the boat, manned

by five very unmilitary looking individuals, came alongside and hooked onto the *Netuno*'s chains. The man at the tiller, who seemed to carry some authority, immediately began shouting at Crawford in Spanish. Crawford replied in French, which produced only a shrug of non-comprehension from the Spaniard. A heated argument in which neither side understood the other then developed. It was not until one of the boat's crew, who spoke broken English, translated, that it became clear to Crawford that the Spaniard, who was the captain of the other vessel, was demanding the surrender of his ship. This was piracy, pure and simple.

Crawford acted quickly, shooting the Spanish captain and the man in the bow of the boat, who then released his hold on the *Netuno*. The boat drifted away, with the rest of its crew taking cover behind the gunwales.

This was the signal for the pirate brig, which had closed to within 50 yards of the *Netuno*, to open fire, using her broadside of five guns. The brigantine was raked from stem to stern with ball and grape, as a result of which most of her prize crew took cover below, leaving only Crawford, a seaman named Frost, the boy seaman Olivine, and the Brazilian captain on deck. Frost took the wheel, while Crawford and Olivine manned the 6-pounders, the Brazilian volunteering to bring up the powder and shot.

The close-quarter action continued for almost two hours, with the two ships sailing bulwark to bulwark, the pirate's five-gun broadside pounding the *Netuno* unmercifully. Most of the brigantine's sails and rigging were shot away and she was holed on the waterline, but throughout Crawford and Olivine continued to man their 6-pounders, returning shot for shot, and to good effect. With darkness coming in, they had only a few cartridges left, when a ball smashed through the bulwark near the guns, and Crawford went down, wounded in the temple by a splinter. The shot also killed a woman on the slave deck and wounded a young girl.

Seeing Crawford go down, Frost left the wheel and took over one of the guns. His first shot scythed through a group of pirates on the other ship's forecastle, and that was the end of the battle. The pirates, already without a captain, had by this time lost more than twenty men to Crawford's guns, and they had no more fight left in them. They deserted their guns, and piling on sail, hauled way from the troublesome little brigantine.

The gallant fight put up by the 75-ton prize-brigantine *Netuno* against vastly superior odds found a well-deserved place in the annals of the Royal Navy. In recognition of his inspired leadership and bravery in action, her commander, Richard Crawford, was immediately commissioned as lieutenant. As for the pirate brig, believed to be the *Carolina*, registered in Havana, she limped away to bury her dead and lick her wounds. A search was organised for her, but she had disappeared back into the murky waters of the Caribbean whence she had come, never to be heard of again.

HMS *Esk*, with Captain William Purchas still in command, left the coast of Africa to return to England at the close of 1827. In the two years she spent with the African Squadron, she had captured nine slavers, Brazilian, Dutch and Spanish, and had been instrumental in freeing 2,249 slaves. But this was only a drop in the ocean. It was estimated that at that time almost 10,000 slaves annually were being exported from the Gallinas area alone.

Chapter Nine

Shortening the Odds

Captain William Broughton

Sacred to the memory of Captain William Broughton who died at Tenby after a short illness on the 17th August 1849 aged 44 years leaving a widow and 6 daughters to deplore his loss. He was the eldest son of Capt. W.R. Broughton CB (who circumnavigated the world with Vancouver) and was an officer highly distinguished in his profession for his services in the Burmese War and for a gallant, skillfully conducted and successful action fought by him in command of HMS Primrose with the Spanish slave ship Veloz Passagera of greatly superior force, on which occasion Capt. Broughton was severely wounded. He subsequently served in command of HM Ships Pearl, Samarang, President and Curacoa. In private life his amiable and generous disposition gained him the esteem of all who knew him.

Memorial in St. Ann's Church, Portsmouth

In 1818, under pressure from Britain, Spain had signed a treaty agreeing to end the participation of all Spanish ships in the carriage of slaves. Included in the treaty were the provisos that, as from 30 May 1820, Spanish ships' captains found to be carrying slaves faced imprisonment for ten years, their ships would be seized, and any slaves on board set free. It was agreed that ships of the Spanish Navy would assist the Royal Navy in the implementation of the treaty. In view of Spain's previous heavy involvement in the slave trade, this seemed to be a bold undertaking by the Spanish Government, but it soon proved to be no more than an empty gesture. The sugar plantations in Cuba could not be worked without a steady supply of African slave labour, and by the simple expedient of re-registering Spanish ships in Havana, the treaty was easily circumvented.

Until this time, the workhorses of the African Squadron had largely been small, lightly armed brigs, capable of working close inshore and penetrating the rivers and creeks, where the slavers gathered their pathetic cargoes. Useful though they were, the brigs were sluggish sailers, handling more like river barges than the ocean hunters they purported to be. In a chase in open waters the slavers, purpose-built for speed, inevitably showed them a clean pair of heels. Determined not to be beaten in this deadly game, some commanders on the spot found their own solution to the problem. Captured slavers were condemned, and either destroyed by burning or sold at auction in Freetown, and in 1826 Commodore Charles Bullen bought with his own money the condemned Dutch slaver *Hoop*. She was a schooner with fine lines, armed with four 18-pounders and one 12-pounder. Bullen optimistically renamed her *Hope*, manned her with his own men, and took her into service as tender to his flagship HMS *Maidstone*. With Lieutenant William Tucker in command, the schooner very quickly repaid Bullen's faith in her.

On 6 September 1826 the *Hope* was off Whydah when Tucker received word that twelve vessels were in the port awaiting cargoes of slaves. Tucker moved back out to sea until the *Hope* was out of sight of the land, and waited. A few hours later the Spanish-owned brig *Principe de Guinea* sailed from Whydah, and Tucker gave chase. He was not aware at the time that the Spaniard was reputed to be the fastest ship on the West African coast, nor that she outgunned the *Hope* by a factor of two to one.

The chase lasted for twenty-eight hours, but by skilful tacking Tucker finally had the brig within range of his 18-pounders. The battle that followed raged for two and a half hours, during which *Hope* had two of her guns put out of action. When this happened, Tucker would have been justified in ending the encounter, but in the best traditions of the Royal Navy he decided to take the fight to the enemy at close quarters. Laying his ship alongside the *Principe de Guinea*, he sent away a boarding party led by his first lieutenant Robert Pengally. Although he was wounded on boarding, Pengally led such a ferocious attack that the Spaniards, who outnumbered *Hope*'s men, lost all stomach for the fight, threw down their weapons and called for quarter.

The *Principe de Guinea* was found to have 587 slaves on board, three of whom had been killed and eleven wounded in the fighting. Casualties amongst the slaver's crew were thirteen killed and twelve wounded, while *Hope* suffered only three men wounded.

The schooner *Black Joke*, tender to the frigate HMS *Sybille*, was another example of a poacher turned gamekeeper. The *Sybille*, under the command of Lieutenant William Turner, a prize taken from the French Navy in 1794, had long since lost her ability to chase, but the *Black Joke* soon made up for her deficiency. Originally sailing under the name *Henrietta*, the schooner had been captured by HMS *Sybille* with 584 slaves on board on 29 September 1828. Armed with one long 18-pounder mounted on a swivel and one long 18-pounder carronade, she had a fast turn of speed, and with a fair wind was capable of overhauling the best on the coast. She carried a complement of forty-four, and was commanded by Lieutenant Henry Downes, supported by an experienced master's mate Edward Butterfield, who was the second son of Rear-Admiral William Butterfield. Although she was comparatively lightly armed, the *Black Joke* quickly became the scourge of the Spanish slavers in the Gulf of Guinea.

Among the *Black Joke*'s more notable conquests was the brig *El Almirante*, sighted in the Bight of Benin on 1 February 1829. Convinced that she was a slaver, Lieutenant Downes gave chase, even though it was obvious that his quarry was a vastly superior ship in all respects. The winds were light and variable, at times hardly enough to fill the schooner's sails, and Downes had to resort to using sweeps to close the gap on the *Almirante*. The chase lasted for eleven long hours under a blazing sun, and the light was going when the *Black Joke* finally came within gunshot range.

Downes put a warning shot across the Spaniard's bow, at which the *Almirante*, armed with ten 18-pounders and nine 4-pounders, replied with a ragged broadside. And so began a desperate, but one-sided, duel, fought at close range. The *Black Joke* was heavily outgunned, and she had the disadvantage of having to avoid hitting the *Almirante* below decks for fear of killing any of the slaves Downes suspected might be chained in the hold. It was also plainly obvious that the Spaniard carried a much larger crew than the *Black Joke*, and Downes was careful not to get too close to her. A boarding would spell disaster for the British ship. He kept his distance, *Black Joke*'s gunners making every shot count. The Spaniard's gunners, on the other hand, although they put up a fierce barrage, wasted much of their shot.

The running fight went on well after dark, until the *Black Joke*'s steady and accurate shooting had carried away much of the *Almirante*'s sails and rigging and created havoc on her deck. She finally surrendered when fifteen of her crew lay dead and thirteen wounded. The *Black Joke* suffered six men wounded, two of whom later died. When the *Almirante* was boarded, 466 slaves were found battened down in her hold.

The following report appeared in the London Gazette on Friday 17 April 1829:

Admiralty Office April 16

Commodore Collier has transmitted to the Right Hon. John Wilson Croker a letter from Lieutenant Henry Downes, commanding the *Black Joke*, tender to His Majesty's ship *Sybille*, reporting that on the 1st February last, the *Black Joke* captured on the coast of Africa, after a long chase and a gallant action, a Spanish slave vessel called the *Almirante*, with 466 slaves on board.

The *Black Joke* carried two guns and 55 men; the *Almirante* 14 guns and 80 men; and Commodore Collier expresses in high terms his sense of the gallant and skilful conduct of Lieut. Downes, and of the zeal and courage of the officers and men under his orders, in this successful action against a vessel of very superior force.

The Spanish vessel had 15 killed, including her captain and first and second mates, and 13 wounded.

The following is a return of the loss on board the *Black Joke*:

Mr T.P. Le Hardy, Admiralty Mate, wounded.

Mr Richard Roberts, Mate (of His Majesty's ship *Medina*), wounded.

Thomas Barley, gunner's mate, wounded.

John Byatt, able seaman, wounded.

Jeremiah Johnson, able seaman, wounded, since dead.

James Allyett, able seaman, wounded, since dead.

Some idea of the conditions prevailing aboard the Spanish slavers at the time may be gained from a report written by the Reverend Robert Walsh in May 1829. Walsh was serving in the 28-gun frigate *North Star* when she stopped and boarded a suspected Spanish slaver.

The first object that struck us was an enormous gun, turning on a swivel, on deck – the constant appendage of a pirate; and next were the large kettles for cooking, on the bows – the usual apparatus of a slaver...When we mounted her decks we found her full of slaves. She was called the *Feloz*, commanded by Captain Jose Barbosa, bound to Bahia. She was a very broad-decked ship, with a mainmast, schooner rigged, and behind her foremast was that large, formidable gun, which turned on a broad circle of iron, on deck, and which enabled her to act as a pirate if her slaving speculation failed. She had taken in, on the coast of Africa, 336 males and 226 females, making in all 562, and had been out seventeen days, during which she had thrown overboard 55. The slaves were all inclosed under grated hatchways between decks. The space was so low that they sat between each other's legs and were stowed so close together that there was no possibility of their lying down or at all changing their position by night or day. As they belonged to and were shipped on account of different individuals, they were all branded like sheep with the owner's marks of different forms...The officers insisted that the poor suffering creatures should be admitted on deck to get air and water. This was opposed by the mate of the slaver, who, from a feeling that they deserved it, declared they would murder them all. The officers, however, persisted, and the poor beings were all turned up together. It is impossible to conceive the effect of this eruption – 517 fellow creatures of all ages and sexes, some children, some adults, some old men and women, all in a state of total nudity, scrambling out together to taste the luxury of a little fresh air and water. They came swarming up like bees from the aperture of a hive until the whole deck was crowded to suffocation from stem to stern, so that is was impossible to imagine where they could all have come from or how they had been stowed away...

The Reverend Walsh did not record what happened to the Spanish slaver, but there were reports that the same ship, with her armament greatly increased but under the same captain, was still engaged in plying her disgusting trade over a year later.

On 6 September 1830 the 18-gun sloop HMS *Primrose*, commanded by Captain William Broughton, was on patrol in the Gulf of Guinea. Broughton, who had taken command of the sloop only four days earlier, had as his first lieutenant Edward Butterfield, ex-master's mate of the *Black Joke*, who had been commissioned following the capture of the *El Almirante*. The weather at the time was not good, with thundery squalls seriously reducing visibility, but when at 4 o'clock that afternoon a sail was sighted on the horizon, Broughton, no doubt anxious to prove himself, immediately gave chase.

The *Primrose* had a good turn of speed, but try as he might, Broughton was unable to overhaul the strange sail. By the time the sun went down, the gap between the two ships was growing wider, and by nightfall the stranger was out of sight. Broughton was now convinced that the other ship was up to no good, and he refused to abandon the chase, pressing on under full sail. His perseverance was rewarded soon after 10 o'clock, when the moon came through a break in the clouds, and a lookout in the crosstrees hailed the deck. There was a sail in sight dead ahead.

Another hour, and the *Primrose* had closed the gap on the strange ship. Broughton now recognised her as the Havana-registered slaver Freetown had warned him to look out for. He hoisted his colours, then fired a warning shot across her bows. The Spaniard hove to and ran up her own ensign. As soon as they were close enough Broughton hailed her, demanding to know her name and where she was bound. The reply came back, '*Veloz Pasajera*, bound St. Thomas for wood and water.' This confirmed Broughton's suspicions, and he sent away a boarding party to search the Spaniard.

Lieutenant Butterfield was in command of the boarding party, and as soon as he set foot on the deck of the *Veloz Pasajera* he realised he was not welcome. The Spaniard had a crew of around 150, all of whom appeared to be armed to the teeth and not attempting to conceal their hostility. He also noted that the gun ports were open and all guns manned. It seemed that the *Primrose* might have taken on more than she could manage.

The Spaniard's captain was not on deck to receive Butterfield, but when he was persuaded to put in an appearance, he gave his name as Jose Antino Barbozo. At first Barbozo seemed willing to cooperate, but when Butterfield said he wanted to search the ship, his attitude changed abruptly. He refused point blank to allow any inspection of his hatches or accommodation. When Butterfield insisted, Barbozo became openly belligerent, as did his crew, who had gathered around fingering their weapons. The message was obvious, and as the *Veloz*'s broadside of ten guns was plainly trained on the *Primrose*, now close on the beam, Butterfield decided to return to his boat and report back to Captain Broughton.

With Lieutenant Butterfield and his party back on board *Primrose* empty-handed, Captain Broughton decided to make one last attempt to reason with Barbozo. He hailed the *Veloz Pasajera* and through his Spanish interpreter made a forceful request for his men to be allowed to inspect the ship. Barbozo refused, putting forward the excuse that the *Primrose* might be a pirate ship, and that he was not prepared to risk a boarding in the dark. Broughton tried to reassure the Spanish captain, but to no avail. Broughton was tempted to settle the matter there and then, but decided to wait until daylight, when there could be no doubt about the identity of his ship.

The weather was by now fine and clear, and *Primrose* was easily able to keep the Veloz in sight throughout the rest of the night. At first light Broughton hoisted ensigns fore and aft and bore down on the Spanish ship. As soon as he was within range he hailed her, identifying his ship as 'His Britannic Majesty's ship *Primrose*', and demanded that the *Veloz* heave to so that a boat might come alongside. He backed up his demand with the warning that he would open fire if the order was not obeyed within five minutes. Barbozo appeared not to be worried by the threat, and replied that if Broughton opened fire, he would return the compliment.

There was no answer to this, other than for Broughton to open fire; but as the *Veloz Pasajera* was a much bigger ship, and carried more guns and more men than the *Primrose*, the British captain knew he must hit first, and hit hard.

The two ships were now racing under full sail, bowsprit to bowsprit, and with no more than a dozen yards of open water separating them. On Broughton's signal, the *Primrose*'s 18-pounders thundered, raking the *Veloz* with their broadside of hot iron, smashing through her bulwarks, and creating carnage on her deck. The Spaniard immediately replied, her broadside somewhat ragged; but at the point blank range few of her balls missed, and the British brig's scuppers also ran red with blood.

Broughton fired another broadside into the *Veloz*, then put the helm hard over to lay the *Primrose* alongside her. The two ships came together with a crash, timber screeching on timber as they locked and careered onwards. With Broughton in the lead, Butterfield at his side, the British swarmed aboard the *Veloz*, and fierce hand-to-hand fighting broke out, with no quarter given on either side.

Primrose's men were outnumbered, but their tight discipline and fearless aggression soon had the Spaniards falling back. Captain Broughton was seriously wounded by a Spanish pike and fell to the deck, but Lieutenant Butterfield took command, and under his leadership the Spaniards were driven slowly aft. The bitter hand-to-hand fighting raged for another ten minutes, then, forced onto the poop and with their backs to the stern rails, the Spaniards realised the day was lost. They threw down their arms and struck their colours.

When the hatches were thrown open the stench was overpowering, and to Lieutenant Butterfield, unmistakeable. Below, in the darkness of her hold, the *Veloz Pasajera* was hiding 555 slaves, taken on in Whydah from the barracoons of the notorious slave merchant Joachim Gómez. The poor wretches had been destined to suffer the horrors of the Middle Passage, those who survived

109

this ordeal condemned to a lifetime of forced labour on some Spanish plantation in the Americas.

The cost of taking the *Veloz Pasajera* had been high. The slaver lost forty-six men killed, with another twenty wounded, including her captain Jose Antino Barbozo, who had lost an arm in the action. Five innocent slaves were also killed. *Primrose*'s butcher's bill was shorter: only one seaman and two marines killed, and ten others injured. The *Veloz Pasajera* was taken to Freetown, where she was condemned by the court. Her surviving slaves were freed.

Despite the determined efforts of the African Squadron, which suffered from the time-honoured Admiralty disease of over-stretching and under-manning, the slave trade continued to flourish in the Gulf of Guinea. The *Black Joke*, although in an advanced state of decay, was still part of this continuing crusade. In 1831, now under the command of Lieutenant William Ramsey, she was tender to Commodore Hayes's flagship HMS *Dryad*, and had been joined by another ex-slaver, the schooner *Fair Rosamond*. Originally the *Don Amigos*, she carried a similar armament to the *Black Joke* and shared her fast sailing qualities – some said she was even faster. In command was Lieutenant Sir Henry Huntley.

In April 1831 the *Black Joke* lay at anchor in the sheltered waters between the island of Fernando Po and the mainland of Equatorial Guinea, just 50 miles southward of the Niger Delta, temporarily out of work but ready to weigh should a slaver be in the offing. On the morning of the 22nd a British merchantman anchored near by, and her master sent word that a powerful Spanish slave brig was in the Old Calabar River. She was said to be armed with a large swivel gun and four other guns, and carried a crew of seventy, which included a number of British seamen.

Ramsey sailed at once, and by nightfall the *Black Joke* was on station off the entrance to the Calabar River. Over the next three days and nights Ramsey kept watch on the estuary, moving close in at night but retreating back out to sea at daylight to lie just over the horizon with topsails lowered.

Ramsey's patient watch bore fruit early on the 25th, when the slaver was seen emerging from the river. *Black Joke* gave chase, but the slaver – she was the Spanish brig *Marinerito* of 300 tons, mounting five 18-pounders – was very soon hull down on the horizon. She was heading south, possibly to St. Thomas to fill her water casks before crossing the Atlantic.

The two ships were off Fernando Po before, at about 9 o'clock that night, *Black Joke* had shortened the range sufficiently to put a shot across the *Marinerito*'s bow. This was immediately answered by a defiant broadside from the slaver's 18-pounders. The chase went on. The winds were light in the region of Fernando Po, and as the night progressed both ships resorted to using sweeps, the *Marinerito*, with her larger crew, just managing to stay out of range of the *Black Joke*'s 18-pounders.

Eventually the Spaniard's rowers were unable to maintain the pace, and shortly after 1 o'clock on the morning of the 26th *Black Joke* had the slaver within range of her two 18-pounders. Ramsey opened fire, and the peace of the tropical night was shattered by the thunder of guns as the ships engaged in a duel to the death at close range. The *Marinerito* was firing high, wreaking havoc amongst the *Black Joke*'s rigging and sails.

They were now very close, almost within jumping distance, and Ramsey changed over to using grapeshot to inflict maximum damage on the slaver's deck. When the two ships crashed bulwark to bulwark, Lieutenant Ramsey, with Master's Mate Bosanquet at his side, led a party of ten men in storming the Spaniard. They were heavily engaged, hand to hand, with the *Marinerito*'s crew, when the two ships drifted apart, leaving Ramsey and his men stranded. It was only the quick action of 14-year-old Midshipman Hinde in using the starboard sweeps to bring the ships together again, and allow more men to board the slaver, that saved the day. Seeing another wave of armed men swarming aboard their ship was sufficient incentive for the Spaniards to lay down their arms.

One man of the *Black Joke*'s boarding party lost his life, and Ramsey, Bosanquet and five other men were wounded in the fighting, while fifteen of the *Marinerito*'s crew lost their lives. As had been anticipated, when the Spaniard's hatches were opened, her holds were found to be crammed with slaves, 496 in all, of whom twenty-six were already dead from suffocation. More than a hundred others were found to be in such a state that Ramsey landed them on Fernando Po where, he later learned, sixty of these died. The *Marinerito*, with a prize crew on board, was sent to Freetown for disposal by the Court, her surviving slaves being released.

Later in the year, *Black Joke* and *Fair Rosamond*, sailing in company, dealt the slavers another blow. The two schooners were off the mouth of the Bonny River in September, when they surprised two Spanish slavers as they emerged from the river. When they recognised the Navy ships, the slavers, named *Rápido* and *Regulo*, immediately went about and re-entered the river. *Black Joke* and *Fair Rosamond* gave chase, and were very soon overhauling the slavers who, fearing they would be caught with the damning evidence on board, began throwing their slaves over the side as they fled up river to some undisclosed refuge. Some of the poor, helpless wretches, still chained together in pairs, made no attempt to stay afloat, and sank. They were the fortunate ones. Others, who were able to swim, struck out for the shore, but ended up screaming for mercy as the giant hammer-headed sharks that scavenge the mouth of the Bonny River tore them to pieces. Only two survived to be picked up by the Royal Navy.

The chase went on for the best part of an hour, with pursued and pursuers cramming on all sail as they raced up river. Inevitably, both the *Rápido* and *Regulo* ended up by running aground on shallow patches, and both were taken by boarding parties from *Black Joke* and *Fair Rosamond*. When she was boarded, the *Regulo* still had 204 slaves on board; the *Rápido* had succeeded in disposing of all her cargo.

The captured Spanish slavers were brought into Freetown, where Peter Leonard, surgeon to Commodore Hayes in HMS *Dryad*, inspected the *Regulo* before her slaves were landed. His comments on conditions in the ship are worthy of note:

> The small space in which these unfortunate beings are huddled is almost incredible. The schooner is only 130 tons burden, and the slave deck only 2 ft 2 in high, so that they can hardly ever sit upright. The after part of the deck is occupied by the women and children, separated by a wooden partition from the other slaves. The horrors of this infernal apartment – the want of air, the suffocating heat, the filth, the stench – may be easily imagined; although it is remarked that this ship is one of the cleanest that was ever brought into the colony.

The men were bound together in twos by irons riveted around the ankles. On their arrival, these chains were removed, and they appeared much gratified.

The *Black Joke*, now visibly ageing, survived only for one more year, before being condemned by Admiralty surveyors, who reported that her timbers were so rotten that, 'she is not in our opinion a vessel calculated fit for HM service.' The schooner was ordered to be burned, and so ended the career of one of the African Squadron's most successful slave chasers. The *Black Joke*, despite mounting only two 18-pounders, in one year alone had taken twenty-one ships and liberated 7000 slaves. Working with the *Fair Rosamond*, her success was even greater. She would be sorely missed on the West Coast.

On occasions the Royal Navy's slave hunters crossed the Atlantic in search of slavers that had slipped through their net in the Gulf of Guinea. One such was the schooner HMS *Pickle*. Commanded by Lieutenant John M'Hardy, *Pickle* was armed with one long 18-pounder and two 8-pounder carronades, and carried a crew of thirty-nine.

In June 1829 *Pickle* was cruising off the north coast of Cuba, near Havana, when the Spanish schooner *Voladora* crossed her path. While on the coast of West Africa in April of that year, the *Voladora* had been under surveillance by the African Squadron and had been twice boarded and searched, only to be released on each occasion through lack of evidence of slave carrying. Once out of sight of the Royal Navy, she had slipped into Grand Pobo, near Whydah, and loaded a cargo of slaves for the Middle Passage. Lieutenant M'Hardy's report of his meeting with the *Voladora* is on file at the National Archives in Kew.

On the morning of June 5th, 6 am, discovered a strange sail to the eastward. She appearing suspicious, every means were used to disguise ourselves, and to prevent her from suspecting us, until 9.30, when HM schooner *Pickle* was tacked in the chase – upon which, stranger hauled to the wind on the starboard tack, under all sail. At 4.20 pm gaining fast on chase, we showed our colours with a gun. At 6.30 chase having shown no colours, and we having no doubts of our coming up with her in the night, we showed our colours again and fired several shots, that she might not after dark plead ignorance of what we were. At 8.45 we tacked; 8.55 tacked. At 9.15 we tacked again, when the chase tacked and edged away. We now set square sail, and kept to leeward of him. At 11.15 closing fast with chase, down square sail, and fired a shot over him.

At 11.30 chase shortened sail and endeavoured to pass under our stern; hailed him repeatedly, which was answered with musketry and a broadside. We avoided his passing under our stern and commenced firing, aiming principally at his spars; believing him to be a pirate, from the circumstance of his showing no colours, either previous to or during the action. Kept up a continual fire, never out of pistol shot, until 12.50, when enemy's mainmast went, about eight feet above the deck, without a sail standing for and aft. He then hailed to say he had eight killed, captain and seven men wounded, his mainmast gone, that he could now do nothing; he therefore surrendered, saying that he was unable to send a boat aboard.

I then thought it advisable to wait until daylight before taking possession; which being done, she proved to be the *Voladora* (formerly the notorious *Mulata*, of which memorandum is made on her papers by Commodore Collier) commanded by Bonifacio Echelacu, pierced for sixteen guns but mounting two long twelves and two long eighteens, with a crew of fifty-two exclusive of killed, which I believe to be ten, as two died after she surrendered; and with 335 slaves – measuring 94 feet on deck and about 235 tons English, from Popo, coast of Africa.

Not surprisingly, Lieutenant John M'Hardy's initial report did not go into great detail. He later enlarged on it, saying, 'We reserved fire till we were close on her larboard quarter. The scene was now splendid beyond description. The moon had set and a light breeze was blowing. We could just distinguish the figure of the long, low black vessel we were engaging as she moved around us, except when by the occasional blazes from her sides on the discharge of her guns, she was distinctly visible. The action continued within pistol shot for an hour and 20 minutes, at the end of which we had the satisfaction of seeing the slaver's mainmast fall.'

What M'Hardy failed to mention was that the chase went on for eighteen hours, and *Pickle* only managed to come up on the *Voladora* by wetting her sails to catch the fickle light winds and constantly tacking to gain the advantage. He also omitted to say that the slaver's first broadside killed three of his crew and wounded eight others, leaving him with only twenty-eight men to handle the ship and prepare for boarding. It had indeed been a very close-run thing.

After their surrender, Captain Bonifacio Echelacu and his crew were put in irons and herded below into the slave quarters, where they spent some very unpleasant hours experiencing the hell their captives had suffered on the passage. The *Voladora* was taken in to Havana, where she, her crew, and the slaves were handed over to the authorities.

For their conduct in the action against the *Voladora*, Lieutenant M'Hardy was promoted to commander, while his Mate, William Powell, received a commendation.

Chapter Ten

Taking the War Inland

Captain Bird Allen R.N.

Capt. Bird Allen R.N., who in the 38th year of his age died at Fernando Po 25 Oct 1841 while in command of HMS Soudan on an expedition into the interior of Africa.

Memorial in St. Mary's Church, Tenby, Pembrokeshire, Wales

On 26 July 1833, after years of debate and procrastination, Parliament finally gave a second reading to the Slavery Abolition Act, which outlawed slavery in the British Empire. All slaves were to be freed, and their owners paid compensation. And so a line was at last drawn under Britain's participation in the slave trade. William Wilberforce, then aged 74 and worn out by his long years of campaigning, died three days later, comforted by the knowledge that his life's ambition had been achieved.

Britain had given the lead by making a stand against an evil trade which had prospered from the dawn of civilisation, and in doing this she deserved the support and cooperation of all the advanced nations of the world, particularly those with a maritime capability. Unfortunately, there were still too many vested interests involved in the trade. Britain herself had implemented the Act of 1807 in full, using all means available to her, even being prepared, with the aid of a law passed in 1811, to sentence to transportation or death any British shipmaster found to be carrying slaves. This alone was sufficient to deter even the most persistent British slave carriers from engaging in the trade, either under their own flag or that of another country. The American Congress had outlawed the carriage of slaves at sea shortly after

116

the British Act of 1807, but this only persuaded American slavers to switch their ships to the Spanish flag, carrying a nominal Spanish captain, but with an all-American crew. It was not until 1821 that the US Navy sent five ships to the coast of West Africa to cooperate with the Royal Navy's African Squadron, and as we have seen this proved to be a short lived effort. Pressure exerted by senators from the Southern States, where the cotton plantations could not function without a steady supply of slaves, as well as a deep-seated distrust of Britain's intentions, nudged Congress into a change of heart. The American squadron was withdrawn in 1824. In 1829 Congress passed an act under which slave trading was classed as piracy, and therefore punishable by death. This act was not enforced until Abraham Lincoln became president in 1861. Meanwhile, the fast Baltimore clippers sailing under the Spanish flag continued to run the Middle Passage with slaves.

Spain, Portugal and France had all at some time signed treaties with Britain promising to put a stop to the slave trade, but they had colonies in the West Indies and South America whose economies depended on slave labour, and all three governments took no action. Had these nations, along with America, joined Britain in her campaign, then the Atlantic slave trade would probably have been wiped out in the 1820s. As it was, the evil continued to fester for many more decades after that.

By 1840, thanks largely to the efforts of the African Squadron, the annual number of slaves being exported from Africa had been reduced from over 100,000 to around 65,000, but at a very heavy cost to Britain and her Navy. Almost one sixth of the ships of the Royal Navy were involved, with an annual cost to the British taxpayer of £750,000. For the men who manned these ships the cost was even higher. In the 19th century the coast of West Africa, with its unrelenting heat, energy-sapping humidity, and cruel fevers that carried men away overnight, was a world fiercely alien to the white man. In addition to which, the men of the African Squadron faced the hostility of the slave traders, the slave carriers, and often the slaves themselves. And there was yet another enemy to face. One commodore wrote, 'The monotony of the blockade is killing to officers and men...for months at anchor, rolling terribly, thermometer 86 degrees, no change of companions, no supplies of fresh stock, except at long intervals.' Little wonder that the casualty rate was so high in the ships. In 1838, for instance, out of a total complement of 885 men, 118 had died from disease, accident, or in action.

There were some small compensations. Ships were paid £5 for every slave released and £4 a ton for every slave ship captured. And although there were long periods of inactivity, when the chase was on, with all sail set in attempt to catch a fleeing Baltimore clipper, the adrenaline ran high. The satisfaction came at the end of a chase with the sheer joy of the slaves saved from a life of captivity and hard labour. To most of those who sailed with the African Squadron, the job was well worth the risks that went with it.

After thirty-two years and the loss of so many men by the African Squadron, in the autumn of 1840 the Foreign Office in London decided it was time for a change of tactics, from attempting to deny the sea passage to the slavers to cutting off their supply of slaves at source. While it was the African chiefs who rounded up their subjects and sold them into slavery, it was the slave traders, some of them African, but mostly Spanish or Portuguese, who organised the shipment of these poor unfortunate people. While they were waiting for a ship to carry them into a life of forced labour across the ocean, they were kept in barracoons, or 'slave factories', handy to the sea. If these barracoons could be closed down, then the trade would be seriously affected. The first opportunity to put London's plan into operation came in November of that year.

The islands near the mouth of the Gallinas River were one of the principal areas for the assembly of slaves prior to shipment, being home to eight Spanish-owned barracoons, the locations of which were well known to the African Squadron. On the pretext of freeing two black British subjects being held by King Siaca, three ships were dispatched to the Gallinas. They were the brig-sloop HMS *Wanderer* of 428 tons, mounting sixteen guns, the 231-ton sloop HMS *Rolla*, ten guns, and the brig-sloop *Saracen*, 228 tons and ten guns. In command of the squadron was Commander Joseph Denman, who flew his flag in *Wanderer*. *Rolla* was commanded by Lieutenant Commander Charles Hall, and *Saracen* by Lieutenant Commander Henry Hill.

118

Arriving off the mouth of the Gallinas on 19 November, Commander Denman began the operation by blockading the river, and with three ships at his disposal the blockade was complete; no ships entered or left the river for several days. When he judged the conditions to be right, Denman took the three ships across the bar and moved up river to the barracoons, which he found to filled to overflowing with slaves waiting to be taken out to ships. He landed with a substantial armed force and immediately freed ninety slaves, whose owners were trying to smuggle them into the bush. Denman then marched on King Siaca's village, and demanded that the King free the two British subjects he was holding and then sign a treaty abolishing the slave trade throughout his dominions.

Commander Denman was no doubt exceeding the authority given to him by London, but he had seen the opportunity and seized it with both hands. King Siaca, overawed by the threat of Denman's guns, gave in to both demands, and Denman set about destroying the barracoons. Using incendiary rockets, he burned four of the stockades to the ground and freed a total of 841 slaves, whom he put aboard his ships. While he was thus engaged, the local natives ransacked the storehouses attached to the barracoons and made off with everything moveable. The Spanish traders had meanwhile wisely disappeared inland.

The Gallinas River action, which lasted for three days, took a heavy toll of the men of the African Squadron involved. They spent much of the day up to their waists in the stinking water of the mangrove swamps, and their nights were spent in the open under conditions that were not much healthier. Sixteen men went down with malaria, and others were sickening by the time they returned to the ships.

It was estimated that the burning of the barracoons at Gallinas cost the slave traders up to half a million pounds sterling, and that relations between the traders and the locals had been so badly damaged that the slave factories would never flourish on the river again. The Admiralty was so pleased with the outcome of the action that Joseph Denman was promoted to post rank, and he and his men were awarded a special bounty of £4000. However, one of the Spanish traders re-emerged from the jungle with a law suit against Denman, claiming huge damages for the alleged losses he suffered at Gallinas, and the bounty was temporarily withheld. The case dragged on through the courts, and it was February 1848 before a ruling was given in favour of Captain Denman; and the bounty was then paid.

The Gallinas raid was followed by attacks on slave factories along the coast, from the Pongas River to the Congo, causing panic amongst those dealing in slaves. Predictably, with so much money to be made in the trade, the interruption was short-lived. A year later the barracoons had been rebuilt and were once again in business.

In 1500 Pedro Alavares Cabral set out from Lisbon with a fleet of thirteen ships on a voyage to open up India to the merchants of Europe. Adverse winds forcing Cabral's ships further west than he had wished resulted in the accidental discovery of Brazil. Cabral dallied only long enough to claim this new-found land for the Portuguese Crown, before moving on. It was only when colonists arrived in Brazil fifty years later that the potential of this huge country was realised. The rich alluvial soil, when cultivated, was capable of producing enormous crops of coffee, sugar, tobacco, rubber and almost anything else the colonists cared to plant, while it was found that gold, silver and diamonds were all in abundance, waiting to be mined. The only thing that Brazil lacked was labour, and the Portuguese, being founder members of the slave trade, soon solved this problem by importing Africans in great numbers from Angola, their colony on the other side of the Atlantic. As the distance the slaves had to be carried was almost a thousand miles less than the Middle Passage from the Niger Delta to the West Indies, this trade inevitably flourished as the years went by. In the period from 1759 to 1803, the height of the transatlantic slave trade, 642,000 slaves were shipped from Angola to Brazil to work on the plantations and in the mines. It is not surprising that Angola became known as 'the black mother of Brazil'.

One of the first things the British government did when it began its campaign against the slave trade was to try to limit the activities of the Portuguese, who had become dominant in the trade. Eventually, in return for the cancellation of a substantial debt owed to Britain and the promise of compensation for ships seized when slaving, Portugal agreed to confine her slave trade to ports south of the Equator. The real breakthrough came in 1822, when Brazil declared independence. The Portuguese slave trade from Angola then became illegal, thus allowing the Royal Navy to take action against any ships found to be involved.

At dawn on 30 April 1841 HMS *Fantome*, a 16-gun brig-sloop of the African Squadron operating south of the Equator, was off the coast of Angola in the region of Ambriz. In command of the 483-ton *Fantome* was Captain Edward Butterfield, who had distinguished himself in the fight against the slave trade while he was mate of the *Black Joke*, and later as first lieutenant of HMS *Primrose*. Twelve years on the coast of West Africa pitting his wits against the wily slavers had given Butterfield a keen eye for one of their kind, and when the first rays of the rising sun showed a strange sail on the horizon, he immediately gave chase.

Butterfield was not aware that he was in pursuit of the Portuguese-owned brigantine *Josephine*, one of the legendary Baltimore clippers and reckoned to be 'the fastest slaver out of Havana'. She had already been chased in turn by four other ships of the Squadron, *Wolverine*, *Bonneta*, *Cygnet* and *Lyra*, all of whom failed to catch her. But the *Fantome* was also built along clipper lines, having been designed by the naval surveyor Sir William Symonds. With all sail set, including the fore and maintop studding sails and the main royal flying jib, she was soon logging 11 knots.

By afternoon, it seemed that, yard by yard, *Fantome* was gaining on the *Josephine*, then Butterfield saw the brigantine cut away both her anchors and jettison a heavy gun in a desperate attempt to lighten ship. The sacrifice of such vital equipment seemed to pay dividends, for the Portuguese ship began to pull ahead again.

From then on, it was a game of skill played between two very experienced seamen, Butterfield and the master of the *Josephine*, who was an American. They proved to be well-matched, but by the time the sun went down, through judicious trimming of his sails, Butterfield had reduced the distance between the two ships to 6 miles.

Disaster almost struck in the early hours of next morning, when both ships, carrying every scrap of sail they possessed, raced through the night under the light of the moon. Butterfield noted

121

in his log: 'At 1 a.m., I took in studding sails and main royal and carried through a tremendous squall of wind and rain – a thing I should never have attempted in any other vessel; and gallantly she went through with it. The slaver was very nearly lost. The *Fantome* kept on gaining on her prey by moonlight.'

When daylight came again, the ships were off the island of Annabona, 190 miles west of Cape Lopez, and within gunshot range of each other. Butterfield put two warning shots close to the *Josephine*, which was enough for her to haul down her colours and heave to. The chase had lasted twenty-four hours, during which the two ships had covered 257 miles, averaging almost 11 knots throughout. When she was boarded, the *Josephine* was found to have 200 slaves on board. Butterfield put a prize crew aboard and sent her to Freetown to be dealt with by the court.

While *Fantome* was engaged in running down the *Josephine*, 700 miles to the north another ship of the African Squadron, the 319-ton brigantine *Dolphin*, was keeping a lonely vigil in the Bight of Benin. Commanded by Lieutenant Edward Littlehales, the *Dolphin* was coming to the end of what was her third month of monotonous patrolling in these sultry, fever-ridden waters, three months that had yielded nothing significant in the unending war on the slavers. The sheer, mind-destroying boredom of the patrol was breeding unrest on board, soon likely to be aggravated by a shortage of food and fresh water. On the morning of 30 May, Littlehales, despairing of ever bringing the enemy to action, was considering putting in to Accra for supplies, when a strange sail was sighted to the south-west. *Dolphin* immediately altered course to intercept.

Seen through the long glass, the stranger appeared to be a nondescript brig with no big guns mounted, and Lieutenant Littlehales assumed she would not offer any resistance when challenged. She was, in fact, yet another Baltimore clipper, the Brazilian brigantine *Firmé*, owned by Jozé Maria Henriquez Ferreira of Bahia, a well known slave trader.

More than an hour elapsed, with the *Dolphin* under full sail in pursuit of the *Firmé*, before the gap between the two ships began to close. By now the wind, which had been blowing fresh, was dying away, and Littlehales judged the time was right to put his boats to work. *Dolphin*'s cutter and gig were lowered, and went away under the command of the mate, Mr. Murray. It promised to be a routine stop and search operation.

Littlehales followed the progress of his boats from aloft, and observed them hoist their colours as they approached the *Firmé*, this being standard procedure when boarding. The Brazilian did not show her own flag in response and heave to, but as *Dolphin*'s boats moved in to go alongside, puffs of smoke erupted from the *Firmé*'s near bulwarks, and Littlehales heard the rattle of musket fire. The boats disappeared from his view when the other ship spilled her wind and changed tack, and he assumed Murray and his men had boarded and taken her.

The *Firmé* had indeed been taken, but when the boats returned to *Dolphin* at 12.30, Littlehales was horrified to learn that the 'routine' boarding operation had turned into a blood-bath. Fired on at close range as they were preparing to go alongside the brigantine, the boarding parties had suffered heavy casualties. Two seamen, William Allen and William Jacobs, had been killed outright, while Murray and another seaman, John Smith, had received very serious injuries. Two other men were slightly wounded. Despite this setback, discipline in the boats had held. The ship was stormed and taken, two of her crew being killed in the fight and seven injured.

When Littlehales boarded the *Firmé*, he found that although she carried no slaves, she was fully equipped for the trade. A slave deck was laid fore and aft, there was a large iron boiler for cooking on the main deck, and below were ninety water casks and a large amount of coarse flour and jerked beef. She was no innocent merchantman. When questioned by Lieutenant Littlehales, her master, Silveiro de Brito, and the supercargo, Jeronimo Carlos Salvi, admitted that the *Firmé*, with a crew of seventeen and ten passengers, was on her way from Bahia to Whydah to pick up a cargo of slaves. The mate, Jozé Ferreira Diaz, who was at the helm when *Dolphin*'s boats approached, said that the crew, against the captain's orders, had broken open the arms chest, which contained twenty muskets, and opened fire on the British boats. Two explanations were given for the crew's conduct, firstly that they thought the boats contained pirates, and secondly that they feared they would lose their wages if the ship was taken.

With the *Firmé* on her way to Freetown with a prize crew on board, the *Dolphin* continued her monotonous sweeping of the Bight of Benin. On 2 July she chased and boarded the Portuguese schooner *Dores* which was found to be partly equipped for slaves. On the following day *Dolphin* made a rare arrest, that of the schooner *Little Grace*, registered in Sierra Leone and flying the British flag. She was also found to be partially fitted out for slaves. Both ships were sent to Freetown with prize crews.

On 7 August *Dolphin* was passing close inshore near Accra, when she sighted a schooner at anchor. Littlehales took his ship in to investigate the stranger, discovering that she was the schooner *Dores* he had captured five weeks previously. When the *Dores* was boarded again, it was found that two of her prize crew, William Penny, gunner, and James Kairns, able seaman, were dead, as was the schooner's master, all carried off by a fever which had broken out on board.

The *Dolphin*'s mate, Mr Murray, having recovered from his wounds received in action with the *Firmé*, was given command of the *Dores* to take her to Freetown. His prize crew consisted of two seamen and three boys, all that Littlehales could spare. Given fair weather, the 900-mile voyage should not have been too arduous, even for such a small crew.

When they boarded the schooner, the new prize crew found her to be in a dreadful state, her sails and rigging worn, and her only accommodation, a tiny cabin amidships, filthy and crawling with vermin. Anticipating a sea passage of ten days or so, Murray set up an awning on deck, under which he and his crew would sleep.

The voyage seemed doomed from the start. With light, fitful winds and a current running against her, the *Dores* made little progress for the first four days, at the end of which she ran into a fierce storm that all but swamped her.

This set the pattern for the rest of the passage, storm after storm sweeping down on the little schooner, and in between each storm, calms or light airs. Out of sight of the land, with no chronometer, no sextant, and a compass of doubtful accuracy, Murray had great difficulty in fixing his position. Twice he found himself blown back to Cape Coast Castle, each time being forced to beg those on shore for food and water to keep his men alive.

The *Dores* had been four months at sea, and had progressed no more than 100 miles to the west, when she faced her greatest challenge. Two violent storms followed one on the heels of the other. W.H.G. Kingston wrote:

...at the commencement of the second [storm], Mr. Murray sent the men below, and remained alone on deck, which he never expected to leave alive. The heat of each flash of lightning was felt as if from a fire; the rain falling in torrents, leaked in every direction through the deck, and the schooner was fast filling with water. At length the rain ceased, and the lightning became fainter, when they made sail again, pumped out, and proceeded till they had made sufficient northing for Sierra Leone. They then bore up east, and, on the 31st December, the colour of the water showed that they were nearing the land. On this day they kept their Christmas, and many were the hearty toasts they drank to those at home.

The *Dores* anchored off Freetown on 6 January 1841, having been at sea for 146 days. Needless to say, she had long since been posted missing, believed lost.

Dolphin, meanwhile, faced another six weeks patrolling the Bight, during which she met up with only a few British ships on legitimate business. Then, on 22 September she was ordered back to the Nun River, where she was to act in support of the Niger River Expedition.

The Niger River Expedition sailed from Freetown on 23 June 1841 in three specially built iron paddle steamers, Her Majesty's Ships *Albert*, *Soudan* and *Wilberforce*. They carried a total complement of 300, including scientists, doctors, missionaries, naval officers, and various other emissaries. The purpose of the expedition was to 'explore the Niger River and introduce Christianity and commerce to the interior of Africa.' In reality, it was another attempt to put a stop to the slave trade at source by persuading the chiefs along the river to sign anti-slavery treaties.

The expedition, which entered the River Niger on 10 September, was under the command of Captain Trotter RN, who was advised by Commander William Allen. Commander Allen had previously explored the Niger, reaching as far as the town of Rabba, home of the Muslim Filatahs. Of the latter, he said, 'Their whole occupation is slave-catching and selling; they make excursions every year during the dry season into the neighbouring states to take slaves. All the tribes have to pay a certain sum as a tribute. Frequently the sums are so great that they cannot pay, and they then seize the people as slaves.' Rabba had become one of the main slave-gathering centres on the Niger, from which slaves were sold mainly to Spanish and Portuguese traders for transport to the Americas, and also to the Arabs, who then took them overland to Tripoli.

Although Commander Allen had navigated the Niger before, this was still a voyage into virtually unknown waters for the three paddle steamers. They had no pilots and no charts, other than a few sketches Allen had made on his previous visit. Consequently, their progress up river was largely a matter of dead reckoning and rule-of-thumb seamanship. They were stemming a 3-knot current all the time, and there was little margin for error; a few spokes of the wheel the wrong way and the ship was caught by the current and slammed into the bank, or brought up short by a hidden sandbank. They moved by day only, with frequent stops to take on firewood; at night they anchored in midstream, or tied up to the bank. But the pitfalls of river navigation were only minor difficulties compared with the threat posed by the swarms of mosquitoes that emerged at night from the mangroves on either side.

Fever struck on the first day in the river, and the first death occurred on the 12th. William Loney, Assistant Surgeon in the *Wilberforce*, wrote in his journal:

It was a trying day to the sick of all vessels. A fiercely burning sun, the air close and sultry, with the thermometer 90° at noon in the shade, and scarcely below 85° even at night, raised the fever to its height; and it seemed with several, that without continued artificial ventilation by fans and frequent cold spongings, they would have expired under the oppression of breathing and heat of the skin. Many of those not yet entered on the sick list were evidentally beginning to feel weak and apprehensive.

In addition to the enervating fever, we seem to be threatened with another and more singular visitation, not less dreaded by the seamen. For the last two nights, the little tenement on the starboard sponson – which having been comfortably fitted up by Lieutenant Strange for some of the blacks, went by the name of Kru Town – had been disturbed by unwelcome intruders in the shape of snakes, which were now abundant in the water, being driven off the high grasses on the inundated islands. The fear of these – as some were said to be venomous – was certainly one of the horrors, and in all the vessels several were killed at night, having either twisted themselves up by the cable, or by the paddle wheels.

17th September. For the last three days, the fever had been progressing rapidly in all the vessels, and in the little *Soudan* only six persons were able to move about, and these showed evident proofs, by depression of spirits and lassitude, that the dreadful climate was too surely doing its work. Lieutenant Ellis, Mr Marshall, Mr Waters, and several of her crew are in a most dangerous state. On board the *Albert*, Mr Nightingale, the assistant surgeon, was at the point of death; and several in the *Wilberforce* in almost as hopeless a state. The scenes at night were most agonizing. Nothing but muttered delirium, or suppressed groans were heard on every side on board the vessels, affording a sad contrast to the placid character of the river and its surrounding scenery.

By the 18th the malaria had swept through the three ships reaping a fearful harvest. Seven men had died, and another sixty were severely ill. It was the opinion of Assistant Surgeon Loney that nearly all the other members of the expedition were showing symptoms of the fever. Drastic action was needed, and after consulting with the surgeons, Captain Trotter decided to send all sick men that could be moved back down the river to the open sea, where they might have a better chance of survival. He ordered the *Soudan* to make ready to return down river to rendezvous with the *Dolphin*, which it was hoped was waiting to give support. William Loney's journal describes the departure:

Sunday 19th. The *Soudan* came alongside the *Wilberforce* to receive our invalids, who took a melancholy farewell of their officers and messmates.

Prayers were read to the crews of both vessels. It was an affecting scene. The whole of one side of the little vessel was covered with invalids, and the cabins were full of officers; there was, indeed, no room for more.

The separation from so many of our companions under such circumstances could not be otherwise than painful to all; the only cheering feature was in the hope, that the attenuated beings who now departed would soon be within the influence of a more favourable climate, and that we might meet under happier auspices.

In a short time the steam was got up, and our little consort – watched by many commiserating eyes – rapidly glided out of view.

William Loney's hopes for the recovery of the sick men would not be realised for some. *Soudan* arrived at the mouth of the Nun River on the morning of the 22nd, where thirty-seven fever cases were transferred to the waiting *Dolphin*. As soon as they were aboard, the brigantine sailed for Ascension Island. Her log for the passage makes sad reading:

26 Sep Sun a.m.
1.40 Departed this life William Moffat, Sapper and Miner, HMS *Albert*
6 Set flying jib, fore royal and main t'gallant sail. Departed this life Ellis Jones, Quarter-master, HMS *Albert*
8 Committed the bodies of the deceased to the deep with the usual ceremonies p.m.
3.45 Departed this life Corporal Walker, HMS *Albert*
5.30 Mustered at quarters. Committed the body of the deceased with the usual ceremonies

27 Sep Mon a.m.
2.30 Departed this life John Young, Quarter-master, *Albert*
3.40 Departed this life John Mill, Gunroom steward, *Soudan*
6 Committed the bodies of the deceased to the deep with the usual ceremonies
10.30 Departed this life Jas Kirrens, stoker, HMS *Soudan* and Wm McMillan, Quarter-master, HMS *Albert*

28 Sep Tue a.m.

4 Committed the body of the deceased to the deep with the usual ceremonies

29 Sep Wed Anna Bon S83°W 58 miles

p.m.

12.10 Departed this life James Whittacker, Quarter-master, HMS *Soudan*

4.30 Committed the body of the deceased to the deep with the usual ceremonies

30 Sep Thu Came to (at Annobon Island)

p.m.

Employed watering

7.10 Boats returned with wood and water. Received during the day 4¾ tons and upwards

9.10 Weighed

1 Oct Fri   1.36° S 5.9° E

8 Oct Fri   8.00° S 10.13° W

9 Oct Sat At single anchor at Ascension

10 Oct Sun Discharged the invalids of HM steamers *Albert*, *Soudan* and *Wilberforce*...to the hospital

Having completed her mission of mercy, *Dolphin* returned to the Bight of Benin, where over the next twelve months she apprehended a number of ships either engaged in or fitted for the slave trade. On 4 May 1842 Commander Littlehales was relieved by Lieutenant A. Cumberland, who in turn was relieved on 22 July by Lieutenant Phillip Bisson. A sad footnote was written in her log when she was returning to Portsmouth two months later, having spent more than two years on station with the African Squadron:

19 Oct Wed a.m.

3.30 Departed this life Lieutenant and commander Philip Bisson.

10 Committed the body of the much lamented, and late Lieut P. Bisson to the deep with the usual ceremonies...Mr G. Collier, 2nd Master read his commission as acting Lt Comdr

and took command of the ship.

HMS *Dolphin* reached Portsmouth on 22 November 1842.

The Niger Expedition, the principal aim of which was to 'prepare the way for commercial enterprise by examining the economic capacity of the adjacent country and making treaties with its chiefs,' failed miserably. Only one treaty was signed and a model farm was set up. Otherwise, nothing was gained, while of the 193 British men who had braved the perils of the River Niger with such high hopes of striking a blow against the slave trade, forty-one had lost their lives.

Chapter Eleven

The Bight of Benin

Commander W.G.B. Estcourt

Sacred to the memory of Commander W.G.B. Estcourt, late in command of Her Majesty's Steam Sloop Eclair, who died on 16th September 1845 aged 38 years on passage from Bona Vista to Madeira from fever contracted on the coast of Africa, while employed in the suppression of the slave trade. His brother Officers and friends, to whom he became endeared by his many virtues, have erected this tablet to record the deep sense of their loss, and perpetuate the memory of his worth. With Commander Estcourt perished 65 Officers and Men in the short period of two months.

Memorial at St. Ann's Church, Naval Dockyard, Portsmouth

In all the long years of their campaign to end the slave trade, the men of the African Squadron had always taken great pains to treat their adversaries in a fair and humane manner. Despite their own heavy casualties, they never killed wantonly, and, if they were able, had always given quarter when it was asked for. In return, the slavers had a grudging respect for these policemen of the sea. All this was about to change.

On 24 July 1845 the Crown Court at Exeter was the scene of a trial then unprecedented in the history of the English courts. Presiding was Mr Justice Baron Platt, and on trial were Janus Mayaval, Francisco Fereira De Santa Serva, Manuel Jose Alvar, Sebastian De Santos, Manuel Antonio and Jose Antonio. The *Monmouthshire Merlin and South Wales Advertiser* reported that:

Much excitement prevailed in the city. Every precaution, however, was taken by the High Sheriff to prevent the court being too crowded, and to condure to the convenience of all parties connected with the case, and also to the reporters. Crowds of persons assembled around the court at an early hour, and the galleries of the court were filled long before the learned judge took his seat, with all well-dressed persons and many ladies.

The trial had its origins in the Bight of Benin some five months earlier when, on the morning of 27 February 1845, the 18-gun brig-sloop HMS *Wasp* was patrolling 50 miles to the south of Lagos. Late February is the start of the rainy season in the Gulf of Guinea, and the winds were characteristically light and variable. Overhead the sky was clear and blue, but from the land, where the dark cumulo-nimbus clouds were beginning to bubble up, there came the distant rumble of thunder. To Commander Sidney Ussher, commanding the *Wasp*, it seemed that this was to be just another hot and sultry day, marked only by the tedium of endless tacking to and fro in search of the elusive slavers. The waiting finally came to an end in mid-morning, when a strange sail was sighted ahead. Ussher needed no urging to give chase.

It soon became evident that the stranger was a two top-sail schooner, typical of the Spanish and Portuguese slavers frequenting these waters, and very likely the same ship that had given *Wasp* the slip several times in the past weeks. *Wasp* was a notoriously slow sailer in anything but a strong breeze, and in the light winds then prevailing there seemed little chance that she would be able to overtake the schooner. However, Ussher had a distinct advantage over his quarry. His men were well drilled in trimming sails to gain the most out of every breath of wind.

By the time the sun was overhead, Ussher judged he was close enough to the schooner to be able to send his boats away. The gig and cutter were lowered, and set off with a fifteen-strong boarding party. Lieutenant Robert Stupart in the cutter was in overall command, while Midshipman Thomas Palmer was at the helm of the gig.

Stupart's instructions were concise. He was to board and search the stranger, and if she had slaves on board, or was visibly equipped to carry them, then he was to detain her. In view of the fact that his boarding party was armed with only two pistols and five cutlasses, all that *Wasp*'s gun chest would run to, this was more than ambitious. Furthermore, if the schooner really was engaged in slaving, her crew might be armed to the teeth and unwilling to allow their ship to be searched. Lieutenant Stupart's mission was not without risk of failure.

It was almost 8 o'clock that night before the boats caught up with the fleeing schooner, which gave Stupart plenty of time to work out a plan of action. In the event, when the boats did finally lay alongside the schooner, he threw caution to the winds and led his men up the ship's side and over her bulwarks in typical Navy style.

Surprisingly, in view of the few arms they carried, the boarding party met with no resistance when they reached the deck of the schooner. She was, Stupart discovered, the Brazilian ship *Felicidade*, and carried a crew of twenty-eight, all of Spanish or Portuguese extraction. Her captain, Joaquim Antonio Cerquira, 'a most forbidding-looking man, short, slight and very dark coloured,' protested against the boarding, but agreed to his vessel being searched. There were no slaves on board, but even though it was dark, and very few lanterns were available, it soon became evident that the *Felicidade* was fitted out for the trade. In her hold she had planks laid fore and aft, and when these were lifted, the space below contained typical slave provisions, bags of farina and casks of water. When questioned, Cerquira said he had sailed from Brazil on 6 January and had arrived on the coast of Africa a month later. After some prompting, he admitted that the purpose of the voyage was to pick up a cargo of slaves at Luanda and take them back to Brazil. However, when the *Felicidade* arrived, the slaves had not yet reached the coast, and Cerquira had been instructed to wait in the vicinity of Lagos until his cargo was ready. He told Stupart that he had several times been chased by British men of war, including the *Wasp*, and had always escaped by virtue of the *Felicidade*'s exceptional sailing qualities. It emerged that on this occasion he had only been caught because he had a boat on shore, and was reluctant to run away and leave it.

Wasp and the *Felicidade* kept company during the rest of the night, and next morning all but seven of the Brazilian's crew were transferred to the *Wasp*. When the transfer was complete, Commander Ussher instructed Lieutenant Stupart to take the *Felicidade* to Freetown for the adjudication of the court. The two ships then went their separate ways.

On the morning of 1 March, *Felicidade* sighted a brigantine, which Stupart thought he recognized as a regular slaver, and he gave chase. The ships seemed evenly matched for speed, and it was 10 o'clock that night before the *Felicidade* caught up with the other ship, by now identified as the Brazilian brigantine *Echo*. She obligingly took in sail to allow the *Felicidade*'s jolly boat to come alongside, but as soon as the Brazilians realised the boat contained a British naval boarding party, they immediately spread all sail and ran away.

Retrieving his boat, Stupart resumed the chase, and another six hours elapsed before he was within hailing distance of the *Echo* again. This time, he threatened her with the *Felicidade*'s guns, and ordered her to lower her sails. The Brazilian complied, and Stupart boarded her. Her captain, one Francisco Fereira De Sante Serva, protested that he was on a legitimate voyage with cargo, but the stench coming from the schooner's hold told a different story. When the hatches were opened, 430 slaves were found to be stowed below in the most appalling conditions. Stupart had no hesitation in arresting the ship and her crew.

Robert Stupart now found himself in the unenviable position of being in command of two ships, one with 430 helpless slaves on board, and both with openly hostile crews. His own resources were meagre. At his disposal he had only sixteen men armed with two pistols and four cutlasses – one cutlass having been lost when boarding the *Echo*. He gave Midshipman Palmer command of the *Felicidade*, with nine men to support him. Palmer had a pistol, one of his men a cutlass, and the others had armed themselves with iron bars. In order to even up the number of prisoners in the ships, fourteen of the *Echo*'s crew were sent on board the *Felicidade*; seven of these Palmer put in a boat and towed astern, supposedly out of harm's way. This left Stupart and his seven men, armed with a pistol and three cutlasses, to look after the *Echo*, her slaves and fourteen prisoners. On the following morning the two ships set sail for Freetown in company. As both prize crews had been without proper sleep for nearly three days and nights, this was a situation fraught with many dangers.

Later that day, while Stupart and his men were handing out food and water to the slaves on board the *Echo*, the *Felicidade* was seen to be bearing down on them. Thinking that Midshipman Palmer wished to speak to him, Stupart shortened sail to allow the other ship to come up.

When the *Felicidade* drew near, Stupart saw that she was again flying a Brazilian ensign, and that there was no sign of Midshipman Palmer or any of his men on deck. Stupart at once suspected that all was not well on the schooner. His suspicions were confirmed when Francisco Serva, ex-master of the *Echo*, hailed him from the *Felicidade*, demanding that Stupart heave to. When Stupart not surprisingly ignored the demand, the *Felicidade* opened fire on the *Echo* with a few rounds of grapeshot. She then suddenly sheered away and sailed off. Stupart went after her, but the *Echo* did not have the sailing qualities of the *Felicidade*, and the other ship was soon out of sight.

There was no doubt in Lieutenant Stupart's mind but that the *Felicidade* had been retaken by the Brazilians, and he feared for the safety of Midshipman Palmer and his men. He also realized that there was now nothing he could do for them. Reluctantly, he resumed course for Freetown, realizing that his only sensible option was to report the incident to the commodore. As for the fate of Midshipman Thomas Palmer and his nine-man prize crew, we must turn to the statement made by Joaquim Cerquira to the court in Exeter. Shortly after boarding the *Felicidade*, Palmer had rounded up all twenty-one prisoners and confined them to the forecastle under guard, with the exception of Cerquira and Francisco Sera, whom he allowed to remain on deck. He then allocated his men to their various duties, and allowed himself the luxury of a bath before returning to the deck. Cerquira, who was already aware that there was a move afoot by the prisoners to take over the ship, testified at his trial in Exeter:

One Englishman was at the helm. I do not know his name. Another was stationed forward, another was lying forward, another was in midship, and one was sentry alongside the hatchway. Three were asleep and one of those was very tipsy.

The sentry by the hatchway was one of those asleep. The quartermaster was talking to Mr Palmer. There were two Kroomen on deck belonging to the *Wasp*. At that time Serva went to the hatchway and called the men to come up. I caught Serva by the hand. I went from aft over to him when I saw him at the hatchway. I said to him, 'Don't be foolish.' Serva was still calling the men to come up. Serva said, 'Come up here, men, come up.' When I saw them coming up, I made a sign to the quartermaster and officer. The quartermaster then caught up a bar of iron, struck prisoner Alves on the head, caught him up and threw him overboard. Alves fell on the starboard side of the deck. The quartermaster struck at him as he was coming up the hatchway with a knife in his hand. It was a knife with a white handle and a long blade. All of them had knives. They could only come up the hatchway two at a time, and Alves was first. Alves had got on deck when he was struck down. The quartermaster caught hold of a handspike after this and began to defend himself from the prisoners, who came on deck, except two or three, who said they were poorly. Antonio Joaquim, Sebastian de Santos and Jose Antonio had no knives in their hands when the prisoner Alves was struck, but they had knives in their belts. Those two did not come up from the hatchway – they were lying on the deck. Antonio Joaquim was also on deck. The other two complained of feeling poorly, but he did not. The other men then came up with their knives and set upon the quartermaster. Four or five came up, but Mayaval was not one of them. Mayaval ran up when called by Serva. The men who came up from the hatchway were Alves, Florenzo Ribeiro, Juan Francisco and Jose Maria Martines. All these had knives. As soon as they came up they fell aboard the quartermaster. He defended himself with a handspike. All the while they were sticking and cutting him with their knives. At this time Serva called the people out of the boat astern. Mayaval now came out of the cabin, where he had been making dough, with a long cooking knife in his hand and went and ran the young officer through the side. He then caught hold of his feet and threw him overboard. After that Mayaval went to assist the others, who were forward. One of the sailors, who was asleep, was killed by one of the crew, who stabbed him in the breast. This man killed himself after he was captured by the *Star*. Mayaval then went forward, and all were cutting and slaying together. One of the Englishmen was thrown partly overboard, and hung by the side of the vessel – this was the sentry; he had caught hold of the fore sheet and held on to it. Antonio Joaquim then went to him and cut his fingers off with his knife and he sank into the water and disappeared. Others of the crew had beaten him over the head with a piece of wood. The quartermaster was killed and thrown overboard. The two Kroomen jumped overboard and I cannot tell what became of them. Serva was standing on deck saying, 'Kill 'em, kill 'em, throw 'em overboard.' After all were killed and thrown overboard, Serva gave orders to lower the peak of the mainsail as a signal to his brother-in-law to rise and kill all the English on board the brigantine. Serva took command of the *Felicidade* and gave orders to hoist the Brazilian flag, which was done, and to chase the brigantine. We came up with the brigantine, the guns having been shifted ready to fire, and all hands stood behind me, and Serva ordered me to fire. I elevated the gun, but another fired it. Serva ordered me to elevate the gun. Serva then ordered me to hail the brigantine to heave to, and he called to his brother-in-law that all the English were dead. I hailed by this order in Portuguese, and told them that all the English were dead. I saw Lieutenant Stupart and Serva's brother-in-law on board the *Echo*. The schooner then sailed on and fired another gun into the bows of the brigantine. Serva gave the order. When Serva found the brigantine did not heave to, he ordered the schooner to be put about and sailed away. Serva said that as he had taken the *Felicidade* from the Englishmen she was his. When we sailed away from the *Echo*, the decks were covered in blood, which it took an hour to wash off...

By this time, Joaquim Cerquira was beginning to realise the enormity of the atrocity he had been party to, and he was desperately seeking a way out. When he asked Francisco Serva where he intended to take the *Felicidade*, Serva replied, 'I am going to Rio de Janeiro, as it is my vessel, taken out of the Englishmen's hands.' Cerquira pleaded, 'I hope you will put me on board the first vessel you meet, as I would rather pay my own passage than remain on board, or put me on the first land.' As it turned out, Cerquira did find passage in another ship, but not one he would have chosen of his own free will.

Four days later, on 6 March, the *Felicidade*, then on a westerly course, was sighted by the 8-gun packet brig HMS *Star*, commanded by Commander Robert Dunlop. Suspicious of the strange schooner, Dunlop gave chase. Serva attempted to escape, but when he found he could not outrun the British brig, he began drinking heavily. He lost all control over his crew, who on the approach of the *Star* lowered the sails, and then concealed themselves below decks. When the slaver was boarded by *Star*'s first lieutenant and an armed party, Serva was the only man on deck and he was very drunk. The ship was searched, and her crew rooted out of their various hiding places. They denied all knowledge of slaving, and insisted that their ship was named *Virginie*, but their odd behaviour, and that of their captain, who was now claiming to be a passenger in the ship, prompted a more detailed search. Suspicious bloodstains were found on deck, which the crew claimed were the result of a spar falling and injuring several of them. This may have been just plausible, but when an English manual of navigation bearing Lieutenant Robert Stupart's name was found in the cabin, the crew of the *Felicidade* were subjected to more rigorous questioning. In the course of this, Serva and one of his Negro servants revealed the story of what had happened to Midshipman Palmer and his men, at the same time claiming that they had nothing to do with the massacre. On hearing the evidence, Commander Dunlop seized the ship and ordered the Brazilians to be put in irons and brought on board the *Star*. The *Felicidade*, with Lieutenant John Wilson and a prize crew of nine on board, then set course for St. Helena, where a prize court had been established.

Soon after parting from the *Star*, Wilson found that the *Felicidade* was damaged below the waterline, and was taking on water at an alarming rate. He continued on course for St. Helena, but in darkness on 16 March, with all sails set, the ship was hit by a violent squall, which threw her onto her beam ends. She straightened up, but slowly started to sink, leaving only her masts and forecastle rails above water, to which Lieutenant Wilson and his men were clinging.

Wilson was aware that he had little time left before the *Felicidade* disappeared below the waves altogether, and he set his men to work constructing a raft. They had only three knives between them, but spurred on by the threat of the ship sinking under them, they cut cordage from the rigging and lashed together spars and planks to form a crude raft. An attempt was made to dive on the wreck for food and water, but this was unsuccessful. Shortly after the raft was finished, the waterlogged hulk of the *Felicidade* gave a last shudder and disappeared beneath the waves.

Lieutenant Wilson was unsure of the exact position of the *Felicidade* when she went down, other than that she was near the Equator and somewhere to the south of Lagos. The makeshift raft had no oars, no rudder, and no means of propulsion other than a scrap of sail they had managed to salvage from the wreck. Fortunately, the prevailing wind was from the south, and there was a weak current setting northwards. Looking on the bright side, Wilson reasoned, all they had to do was to keep the wind astern and eventually they were bound to run into the shipping lane, or end up on the coast somewhere in the Bight of Benin. Of course, that was assuming that they had by then not died of thirst, starvation or exposure, for they had neither food nor water, and most of them were almost naked. The future looked very bleak.

For twenty days the survivors drifted on their half-submerged raft, roasted by the blazing sun during the day and shivering in the chill of the nights. Rain fell very occasionally, and each time just enough was collected to slake their raging thirsts for a day or two more. At times, flying fish obligingly hurled themselves aboard during the night, and these were pounced on eagerly, torn apart and eaten raw, if not alive. Sharks followed the raft day and night, waiting patiently for the meal they knew was bound to come. The brutes were not disappointed, for one by one the survivors began to die.

On 5 April, twenty days after the *Felicidade* went down, the brig HMS *Cygnet*, under the command of Commander Henry Layton, on patrol off the coast near Lagos, sighted the raft. On board were Lieutenant Robert Wilson and five of his men. They were burned almost black by the sun, covered in salt water sores, their bodies wasted through lack of sustenance, their tongues swollen for want of water, but they were still alive. Unfortunately, one of their number was too far gone. He died on the deck of the *Cygnet*.

In the meantime, HMS *Star* had arrived in Freetown, where the *Felicidade*'s crew were handed over to the authorities. During the voyage, Joaquim Cerquira had approached Commander Dunlop and related the full story of the murder of Midshipman Palmer and his prize crew and the seizure of the *Felicidade*. Cerquira's testimony was sufficient to convince Freetown that an act of murder and piracy had been committed on the high seas, a crime too serious to be judged by the local court. And so Francisco Serva and his eight co-conspirators began the long journey north-wards that would end in the Crown Court at Exeter, in the county of Devon.

The nine Brazilians appeared in court at Exeter on 24 July charged, 'That with force and arms upon the high seas, in and upon one Thomas Palmer, in the peace of God and our Lady the Queen, then being in a certain vessel known as the *Felicidade*, did feloniously and wilfully make an assault.'

Lieutenant Robert Stupart, Lieutenant John Wilson and Thomas Lethbridge, corporal of marines, gave evidence against the accused, while Emanuel Rossigré and Sobrina da Costa cor-roborated the testimony of Joaquim Cerquira. After a lengthy trial, three of the prisoners, Manuel Antonio, Jose Antonio and Sebastian De Santos, were acquitted and discharged. The jury found Francisco Serva, Janus Mayaval, Maria Alvares, Florenco Ribeira, Juan Francisco, Jose Martines and Antonio Joaquim guilty of the murder of Thomas Palmer, midshipman of Her Majesty's brig *Wasp*, and seven of her crew. In passing sentence on the seven, Baron Platt said:

> In dealing in this guilty traffic, you might have submitted to the power by which you were captured. But this rebellion against that power amounted to the crime of piracy itself. The particular offence, however, of which you are found guilty, and for which you will suffer, is the deprivation of life – depriving this unhappy young man of his life, by these

cowardly and dastardly wounds dealt behind on this poor young man. His blood is rising up for justice, and demands that the ministers of justice should visit your offence with the utmost punishment. The sentence of this court upon you and each of you is, for this foul murder, of which you have been respectively found guilty, you be taken from hence to the place from whence you came, and from thence, at the usual time, you be conveyed to the place of execution, and that there you be hung respectively by the neck until you be dead.

Strong words, but they were not followed by strong action. The condemned men appealed against their sentence, their counsel pleading that as the *Felicidade* had no slaves on board when she was taken by HMS *Wasp*, and that as Britain had no equipment clause with Brazil, which would allow her arrest if she was found to be merely equipped to carry slaves, the seizure of the vessel had been illegal. In which case, the lawyers for the defence argued, the crew of the *Felicidade* were fully justified in taking back their ship by any means at their disposal – even murder. The appeal court agreed, and Francisco Serva and his six co-defendants were discharged, and repatriated to Brazil at the expense of the courts. The outcome of the case caused understandable uproar in Britain and in ships of the African Squadron, but the decision of the appeal court could not be overturned.

Word of the *Felicidade* massacre was already circulating among the African Squadron when in May 1845 the 10-gun sloop HMS *Pantaloon*, commanded by Commander Edmund Wilson, was in pursuit of a large three-masted ship known to be slaving in the Bight of Benin. The chase lasted for two days, the *Pantaloon* finally catching up with the slaver on 26 May, when she was becalmed 2 miles off Lagos.

Anticipating resistance, Wilson sent away his cutter and two whaleboats, with Lieutenant Lewis Prevost commanding a force of twenty-seven armed marines and seamen. Prevost had one of the whaleboats, while the *Pantaloon*'s master, John Crout, was in charge of the cutter, and her boatswain, Pascoe, was in the other whaleboat.

As the boats approached her, the slaver opened fire on them with her four 12-pounders, using round shot, canister and grape.

Anxious to get in under the guns before they did any serious damage, Lieutenant Prevost urged the boats on, and with the marines returning the slaver's fire with their muskets, the little flotilla raced in.

Still under fire, the two whaleboats went alongside the slaver on her starboard side, and at the same time John Crout put his cutter alongside to port. In the face of a hail of musket balls from above, the boarding parties swarmed up the side of the ship and met the slaver's crew hand to hand. Prevost's men being outnumbered two to one, the fight that ensued on the deck of the slaver was hard and bitter, but with the *Felicidade* in mind they fought like men possessed, using cutlass and bayonet ruthlessly. The slavers were forced back inch by inch, until, with seven of their number lying dead and eight more severely wounded, they finally yielded. Two British seamen were killed, and John Crout, Boatswain Pascoe and five others were seriously wounded.

By the time the year 1846 opened, the African Squadron consisted of twenty-six ships, and its activities were striking hard at the slave trade. Shipping slaves across the Atlantic had become an exceedingly hazardous enterprise, with more and more ships being stopped and seized by the British – and yet the demand for slaves in the Americas was as great as ever, if not greater. In desperation, the traffickers were packing their human cargoes into the ships so tightly that if the conditions under which the slaves had been carried before were bad, they were now completely inhuman. On 14 February, the *Colonial Gazette* reported:

> Information has reached us from the west coast of Africa, that the *Hydra*, steam-sloop, Commander Young, has captured a slaver, on board of which were 1,100 slaves. We believe this is the largest number that has ever been captured on board of one vessel. The bonus to the captors will be considerable. Reports are prevalent of some severe visitations of fever among the squadron; none have reached us other than that some cases of an ordinary nature have appeared on board the *Styx*, steam-sloop, Commander Hornby, at Ascension, on the 20th of December; to which, however, the master, Mr Richard L. Rundle, and seven seamen, have fallen victims. The ship has been very fortunate in having captured three slavers; viz,

the *Regevereder* and *Espiza* (empty) and the *Isabel*, with 352 slaves on board, it is supposed that the three prizes will give the commander £400, and the officers and crew according to their ratings in proportion. When ordered to Ascension they were so reduced from sickness and prize crews that, with the exception of the boatswain, the commander was the only officer who was doing duty, with nine men in one watch, and eleven in the other; the men are now in hospital, doing well. It is supposed Captain Hornby will invalid, and return to England, having suffered severely from fever.

Another example of the new face of the trade was the Brazilian brigantine *Paquete do Rio*, a ship of only 70 tons burden (tons burden – or burthen – being a measure based on the number of tuns, or large casks of wine a vessel was able to carry in her hold). The *Paquete do Rio* had arrived in Freetown in the middle of August 1846 with a cargo of merchandise and rum, and one high-ranking passenger, His Imperial Brazilian Majesty's Vice Consul to Sierra Leone, Mr S.P.M. Campos. Her credentials as a legitimate trading vessel appeared to be impeccable, and although the barrels of rum in her hold caused a few raised eyebrows, the port authorities cleared her to sail southwards. Unseen, she then sailed only a few miles down the coast and anchored off Yawi Bay, an isolated cove just outside the jurisdiction of the Sierra Leone authorities. Here she landed her cargo of spirits in total secrecy. She later returned to Freetown, sailing again on 6 October, bound for Rio de Janeiro with twenty passengers, said to be ex-crew members of slavers seized by the Court.

Soon after sailing from Freetown, the *Paquete do Rio* was stopped and boarded by the brig HMS *Lynx*, but nothing suspicious was found on board. However, as soon as the *Lynx* was out of sight, the Brazilian ship put into another isolated anchorage, where she took on board 549 slaves, together with all the provisions, water and equipment necessary for the Atlantic crossing. With her twenty 'passengers' and ten crew, this tiny vessel now had on board a total of 579 persons, the slaves all being crammed into her small cargo hold. It seems to be nothing short of a miracle that she did not sink under the sheer weight of humanity on board, although this might have been a blessing for the slaves, who were chained together and condemned to a voyage that could stretch to months. If the winds were wrong, it would become a nightmare voyage on which, in any case, at least half of them would die. They were fortunate in that before she was many days out from the coast the *Paquete do Rio* was sighted by HMS *Cygnet*, then under the command of Commander Frederick Montresor. The chase was short, for the Brazilian slaver, her gunwales almost awash, was barely able to make headway. Very soon the *Paquete do Rio* and her cargo were on their way to Freetown to face the courts, and the African Squadron was able to chalk up another victory over the slavers.

Chapter Twelve

The Lagos Expedition

To the memory of the Officers, Seamen and Royal Marines who were killed or mortally wounded in the engagements at Lagos on the West Coast of Africa AD 1851. This tablet is erected by their shipmates and companions in arms.

John G.F. Dyer and Henry H. Hall, Mates of HMS Niger, killed 25th Nov. 1851 Fredk. R. Fletcher Mid: J.N.O. McDonald, Wm. Laws, Fredk. Hunn, Thomas Sutton, James Webb, Thos. Davis, Saml. Pitt, Benjn. Tracey and Richd. Peacock, Seamen. Francis Bone, Thos. Nonely and Wm. Wilson, Royal Mar. Arty., and King George, Krooman of HMS Penelope killed 26th December 1851. Hy. M. Gilham, Master's Assistant. George E. Howell, Gunner and W. Botters RMA, HMS Penelope.
   Mortally wounded, Thomas Richards, Mid. HMS Sampson killed 26th December 1851.

Memorial in St. Ann's Church, Portsmouth

Since early man first learned that an animal skin suspended from a crude mast would move his dugout canoe through the water, wind power had been the main means of propulsion at sea. Over the centuries sail had evolved until it was capable of driving large ships around the world free of cost, often at phenomenal speeds. There were times, of course, when areas of calms and adverse winds rendered the sail impotent, but this was accepted as nature's way. When the steamship first appeared on the scene it faced ridicule from all sides, and none were more vehement in their opposition than the admirals and commanders of the Royal Navy.

The origins of the steam engine, like all great inventions, are subject to controversy, but it is accepted that the English military engineer Thomas Savery patented the first commercially successful steam engine in 1698. Almost a hundred years were to pass before steam made its appearance at sea. In 1783, the Marquis Claude de Jouffroy d'Abbans exhibited the *Pyroscaphe* on the River Saône. She was a large, clinker-built boat with a steam engine that powered two small paddle wheels. The *Pyroscaphe*'s engine turned for only fifteen minutes before breaking down, but it did propel her through the water. There was a long road to travel before the steamship became a feasible proposition, but from the moment the *Pyroscaphe*'s paddles first began to turn, the days of sail at sea were numbered.

It was mainly through the persistence of that brilliant engineer Isambard Kingdom Brunel that Britain's navy finally accepted steam. In 1822 HMS *Comet*, a 238-ton wooden paddle steamer equipped with a 90 horse power Boulton & Watt engine was built at Deptford and taken into service with the Royal Navy. However, the *Comet* was never accepted as a fighting ship, and spent all her days as a tug, towing sailing ships in and out of harbour.

At first, the Admiralty was largely indifferent to the introduction of the steamships into the Navy, unhappy that they burned huge amounts of coal, and would require a network of coaling stations around the world to sustain them. This alone, it was argued, would put an intolerable burden on already overstretched resources. However, even the admirals could not stand in the way of progress, and by 1836 the Navy had thirteen steamers in service. But it was a grudging acceptance, Admiral Sir George Cockburn maintaining angrily that, 'since the introduction of steam vessels I have never seen a clean deck, or a captain who did not look like a sweep.'

The African Squadron received its first steamship in 1832. She was the 365-ton wooden paddle steamer *Pluto*, armed with three guns. It was soon found that with only three accessible coaling stations, Freetown, Fernando Po and Luanda, *Pluto*'s role was strictly limited. After two years with the squadron she was sent home, not returning to West Africa until 1841, being joined on the station by four other steamers a year later.

146

By 1851, forty-three years after Commodore Edward Columbine first arrived on the coast with his two ships *Solebay* and *Derwent*, the African Squadron had reached an optimum level of twenty-four ships. Now, it was agreed, the war against the slave traders of West Africa was all but won. Only one important market for the trade continued to thrive, and that was the Nigerian port of Lagos.

When, in the late 1840s, Whydah was under strict blockade by the African Squadron, King Gezo of Dahomey, who boasted of selling 9000 slaves a year, was persuaded by the British government to turn to the production of palm oil. The transformation from the slave trade to agriculture was achieved without too much upset, the slaves Gezo had once exported in such large numbers being put to work cultivating the oil palms. Equally smoothly, the neighbouring port of Lagos had taken over as the principal point of export for slaves in the Bight of Benin.

The rightful ruler in the Lagos area was King Akintoye, also given to enslaving his fellow Africans. Unlike his neighbour in Dahomey, however, who obtained his slaves by waging war, Akintoye bought his slaves from Yoruba traders, who brought them down in coffles from the remote regions in the north. When, in 1851, Akintoye was overthrown by his brother Kosoko and forced to flee to Badagry, he sent an urgent message for help to the British Consul for the Bight of Benin, John Beecroft, who resided on Fernando Po. In return, Akintoye offered to sign a treaty abolishing the slave trade at Lagos, and promised to enter into legitimate trading with the British. Bearing in mind the importance of the area, not only for trade but also for the advancement of Christianity, Beecroft visited Lagos on 20 November, met face to face with King Kosoko, but received a blunt refusal to cooperate. As a last resort, Beecroft contacted Commodore Henry Bruce, then commanding the African Squadron, who at once offered to mount an armed expedition to Lagos.

Commodore Bruce assembled a squadron consisting of the 378-ton paddle steamer *Bloodhound*, the brigs *Harlequin* and *Philomel*, the schooner *Waterwitch* and the steam tenders *Niger* and *Volcano*. These ships arrived off Lagos on 24 November; and since it was the dry season, and the depth of water was uncertain,

147

Waterwitch went in first to survey the channel leading across the bar, and into Lagos harbour.

The entrance to Lagos harbour is a break in the coast only a half a mile wide, which was first sighted in 1484 by the Portuguese navigator Diogo Cão as he was sailing close inshore on his way south to the Congo. Cão sent a boat in through the opening, and so discovered a deep-water inlet offering excellent shelter for ocean-going ships. The inlet led to a lagoon and, on an island 6 miles from the sea, Cão established a trading post, which he named for Lagos, his home port on the Algarve.

Waterwitch, commanded by Lieutenant Alan Gardner, reported sufficient depth of water for *Bloodhound* to cross the bar, and soon after dawn on 25 November the expedition entered the approach channel to Lagos. In the lead was a gig carrying the Consul, John Beecroft, and flying a white flag. The gig was followed by *Bloodhound*, commanded by Lieutenant Russel Patey, also flying a flag of truce, and the steam tenders *Niger* and *Volcano* towing twenty-one boats containing 306 armed seamen and marines. Captain Thomas Forbes of the *Philomel* was in command of the landing parties. On board *Bloodhound* was ex-King Akintoye and his entourage, presumably to advise. *Harlequin*, *Philomel* and *Waterwitch* remained outside the bar at anchor. Little resistance was expected, and the flotilla was primarily intended as a show of force. However, it appears that Bruce's intelligence must have been faulty, for soon after crossing the bar, the boats came under heavy and accurate musket fire from the shore. King Kosoko had been reinforced by 1000 troops sent from Dahomey by his ally King Gezo, and was not in the mood for parley.

As he was entering under a flag of truce, Commodore Bruce ordered his men not to return the fire, and the flotilla crept through the half-mile wide entrance to the harbour with a hail of musket balls kicking up the water all around them. There were no casualties, but it soon became obvious to the men in the boats that Kosoko's Portuguese advisors must be directing the fire. When they came abreast of Lagos Island, the fire from the shore became heavier, but still Bruce continued to hope that his white flags would be respected. They were not, and when, within sight of Lagos town, *Bloodhound* ran aground, a battery of guns on the island opened fire on her.

With *Bloodhound* hard and fast and under fire, all pretence of parley with the enemy was dropped. Bruce ordered the flags of truce to be hauled down, and the fire from the shore was returned. The range was too far for *Bloodhound*'s 18-pounders, but those boats that were armed with 6-pounder carronades hit back with shrapnel and small round shot, backed up by musket fire from the marines.

The fire-fight raged for over an hour, during which a landing party went ashore with the object of silencing the guns firing on *Bloodhound*. It was beaten back by heavy fire from Kosoko's men, who obviously were several thousand strong. Other landings were made by small parties, one of which succeeded in fighting its way into the town, but was eventually forced to retire, having achieved little other than the burning of some large slave barracoons.

During the night the boats formed a protective screen around *Bloodhound* while she was refloated, and next morning, accepting that he was outgunned and outnumbered, Commodore Bruce decided to withdraw. What should have been a demonstration of the overwhelming power of Queen Victoria's Navy, had ended in a humiliating defeat and had cost the African Squadron two men killed and sixteen wounded.

When news reached London of the failure of Commodore Bruce's expedition, there was uproar in Parliament, followed by demands that a new expedition be mounted to teach Kosoko a lesson. This time, it was urged, the attack must be made in sufficient force to avoid any more loss of face. Flags of truce were not to be considered.

Having virtually been given *carte blanche* by London, Bruce took pains to see that his second expedition against Lagos would not fail. He was of the opinion that the main contributory factor to the debacle of November had been the lack of big guns to support the landings. When he set off again in mid-December, in addition to *Bloodhound*, he had with him the 1091-ton paddle steamer *Penelope*, commanded by Captain Henry Lyster, mounting twelve guns, the second-class frigate *Sampson*, a wooden paddle steamer of 1299 tons, mounting four guns, and under the command of Captain Lewis Jones, the 296-ton wooden

149

screw steamer *Teazer*, with two guns, Lieutenant-Commander Jasper Selwyn commanding, and the iron galley *Victoria*, a rocket boat armed with 12lb and 24lb rockets. These vessels were all shallow draught, and with the exception of *Victoria* all capable of being easily manoeuvred. This time Bruce was determined that his landing parties would not be without artillery support. The attack was planned to take place over Christmas, and would be further supported by a 600-strong force led by Akintoye advancing overland from Badagry.

The squadron arrived off Lagos on 24 December, and immediately boats from *Bloodhound* and *Sampson* moved inshore to reconnoitre the enemy's defences. They were not able to see much without entering the harbour, but newly dug earthworks were visible, indicating that Kosoko's men and their Portuguese advisors had been hard at work preparing a reception. In fact, the whole of the western side of Lagos Island was by then protected by a high mud bank, behind which was a deep ditch. At strategic points, Kosoko's big guns were mounted in batteries of twenty-five behind timber and earth barricades. All potential landing places on the beaches were fouled by double rows of bamboo stakes driven into the sand close inshore. Any assault on Lagos Island promised to turn into a hard and bloody fight.

Christmas Day was spent quietly at anchor, while preparations were made for the attack. There was little sleep for anyone that night, and shortly before dawn on the 26th the attacking force moved in towards the harbour entrance. Captain Lewis Jones of the *Sampson* was commanding the boats, which carried 400 picked men, seamen and marines, all heavily armed, and determined that this time there would be no retreat until their task was completed. No white flags were flying, and the boats were protected by *Bloodhound* and *Teazer*, with the rocket boat *Victoria* bringing up the rear of the flotilla.

As had been anticipated, the boats came under heavy small arms fire from the shore as soon as they passed through the entrance to the harbour, but they pressed on, the enemy's fire being returned by the protecting ships. Then, as the flotilla was approaching Lagos Island, disaster struck. Both *Bloodhound* and *Teazer* ran aground.

With two of the British flotilla's escort ships lying grounded and helpless, Kosoko's men opened fire on them with their 12-pounders. *Bloodhound* replied, but *Teazer* was unable to bring her guns to bear. Once again, as a month earlier, the attacking force found itself at a severe disadvantage, and it was quite obvious that unless the situation was quickly brought under control, the operation might have to be abandoned. Captain Henry Lyster, who was to command the landings, ordered *Sampson*'s boats to attempt a landing in order to spike Kosoko's guns.

At 2.30 pm Lieutenant Thomas Saumarez took his boats in under a hail of musket fire from the shore. The shooting was heavy and accurate, and before they even reached the beach Midshipman Richards was killed and ten men had been wounded. Saumarez drove his men on, but as the boats reached shallow water they ran straight into the lines of bamboo stakes planted to thwart the landing, and could go no further. Led by William Stivey, *Sampson*'s carpenter, men waded ashore with axes and tried to hack a way through the stakes, but the musket fire was now so heavy that Saumarez, himself three times wounded, was forced to call his men back. The landing was abandoned, and the boats retreated out of range.

Bloodhound had by now been refloated, but *Teazer* was still hard aground, and under fire. The whole expedition seemed doomed to failure unless something was done to silence the enemy's guns. Captain Lyster decided on another landing, and this time he would lead. Throughout the rest of the day *Bloodhound*, *Teazer* and *Victoria* laid down a heavy barrage of fire on the Kosoko's gun emplacements. Meanwhile, preparations were being made for the second attack, and the wounded were being ferried back to *Philomel* and *Sampson*, anchored outside the bar.

At dawn next day, a possible landing spot on the north-western end of the island having been decided on, the boats went in again, covered by a continuous hail of round shot, grape and canister laid down by the protecting ships. As they drew near to the shore, the boats came under fire from what was estimated to be at least 1,500 muskets, but now that they were committed there could be no going back. Those first ashore hacked a way through the bamboo stakes, the boats were grounded, and Lyster led his men up the beach straight into the enemy's fire. The hand-to-hand fight that followed was brutal, with no quarter given on either side, but in the face of the raw courage of Lyster's men, the defenders of the stockade finally threw down their weapons and ran.

Wasting no time, for Lyster knew that a counter-attack was inevitable, a party under Lieutenant Corbett was sent in to spike the 12-pounder guns in the stockade. This done, Lyster ordered the withdrawal, but as they fell back on the beach it was found that Kosoko's men had seized one of their boats, killing Gunner's Mate James Webb, who was guarding it. Lyster began distributing the landing party between the remaining boats, but while this was being done, the enemy swarmed out of the bush at the head of the beach, and opened up a withering fire at short range. Midshipman Fletcher and several men were shot and killed, while Commander Hillyar, Lieutenant Williams and many others were severely wounded.

While the desperate rearguard fight was taking place on the beach, HMS *Victoria* had moved closer inshore to support the boats with rocket fire. Unfortunately, in the heat of the battle, with the adrenaline running high, one of *Victoria*'s African seamen let go her anchor. The chain ran out to its full length, and when the boats began to leave the beach, the galley found herself unable to move. Attempts were made to slip the cable, but without success. When Captain Lyster and Lieutenant Corbett boarded to investigate the cause of the problem, *Victoria* had become the target of the firing from the beach, and was taking casualties. Corbett, who had already been wounded while ashore, volunteered to cut the anchor chain with a hammer and cold chisel, and while he was leaning over the *Victoria*'s bow he received five more wounds. Despite this, Corbett went over the bow and hammered at the chain until it was finally cut and slipped. When he was hauled aboard again, he was covered in blood and only partly conscious.

As Captain Lyster was returning to his boat, he too was shot, receiving a musket ball in the back, but he persisted in attempting to retrieve the boat captured by the enemy. It was a lost cause; the beach was now swarming with a howling mob firing their muskets as fast as they could load. With so many of his men killed or wounded, Lyster decided to abandon the boat and withdraw to the *Teazer*, which was still aground.

The taking of Lyster's boat had been observed from the *Teazer*, and when forty or fifty of the enemy were seen piling into the boat and attempting to make off with it, *Teazer*'s gunner fired a rocket. He scored a direct hit on the magazine, and the boat blew up, killing many of those on board. The explosion took all the fight out of the mob on the beach, which disappeared back into the bush. This gave those on board *Teazer* the opportunity to try to refloat the stranded ship. With the exception of 10 tons or so, her coal bunkers were emptied, the coal being dumped over the side, and all her provisions were unloaded into the boats. It then remained only to wait for high tide, which came a couple of hours later. With an extra 3 feet of water and the use of a stream anchor, *Teazer* was hauled clear of the shallows and anchored out of reach of Kosoko's guns for the night.

Now came the reckoning. In the attack on Lagos, which had been only a partial success, fifteen men had lost their lives. Another sixty-three, including Captain Lyster, Commander Hillyar, Lieutenant Corbett and First Lieutenant of Marines J.W.C. Fletcher, had been wounded, most of them severely. During the night the medical officers, Senior Surgeon Carpenter, Assistant Surgeon Walling, Acting Surgeon Barclay and Assistant Surgeon Sproule, all of whom had been involved in the attack, worked untiringly to alleviate the suffering of the injured and dying.

At around 7 o'clock next morning *Teazer* was under way and shifted her anchorage nearer to *Bloodhound* and *Victoria*. A council of war was held on board *Bloodhound*, at which Captain Jones and Captain Lyster, mindful of the casualties already suffered, decided against another landing. Instead, it was proposed to bombard Lagos with all guns available, with the object of driving the enemy out of the town.

The guns roared at 10 o'clock, and the town of Lagos cowered as salvo after salvo of round shot, grape and canister rained down on it. The rockets followed, their fiery tails striking fear into the hearts of Kosoko's men. Buildings were smashed, fires started, and one of *Victoria*'s rockets scored a direct hit on the town's main magazine. There was a massive explosion, and soon the whole town was a sea of flames. This was enough for any defenders left. They fled into the surrounding bush.

Next day a small body of men from *Sampson* and *Penelope*, led by Commander Coote and Commander Gardner, went on shore and spiked and dismantled Kosoko's guns, fifty-seven of which were then loaded into the boats, taken out to sea and dumped in deep water. Meanwhile, Akintoye and his men, who had taken no part in the fighting, were landed on Lagos Island. Akintoye then persuaded the local chiefs to accept him as their king once more. In return for the British help in restoring him to the throne, on 1 January 1852 Akintoye signed an anti-slavery treaty on board HMS *Penelope*. This was the end of the slave trade for Lagos, and it was not long before the merchants were moving in to deal in commodities other than slaves. Lagos became an important trading centre, and in 1861 was annexed as a British colony.

The fall of Lagos to the British guns and the restoration of Akintoye to the throne dealt a severe blow to the West African slave trade. For the Royal Navy it had been a long and bloody road. Since the formation of the African Squadron in 1808, a handful of ships, rarely more than twenty-five and mostly nearing obsolescence, had captured 1,200 ships engaged in the trade, and liberated 140,000 slaves. The cost had been great: around £15 million, a huge sum in those days, probably equivalent to about £700 million today. Added to this, around 1,500 British seamen had lost their lives fighting a war that was really of no consequence to them.

Although by the end of 1852 the supply of slaves from West Africa had dwindled to a mere trickle, there was still a steady demand for labour coming from the huge plantations of the Southern States of America and Brazil. In desperation, the slavers were resorting to ever more devious methods of smuggling the 'black gold' across the Atlantic. The case of the US-registered schooner *Wanderer* was a typical example.

The *Wanderer* was built in 1857 on New York's Long Island for the Lousiana plantation owner Colonel John Johnson, a member of the New York Yacht Club. She was a schooner-rigged yacht of 300 tons displacement, luxuriously fitted out, as might be expected for a man of Johnson's means. However, her cruising days were short. After one voyage to the Gulf of Mexico, the

Wanderer was sold to another Southern gentleman, Captain William C. Corrie of Charleston, South Carolina. Corrie was secretly acting on behalf of a slaving syndicate headed by Charles A.L. Lamar of Savannah. In Charleston the yacht was discreetly fitted out to carry slaves, her equipment including fresh water tanks capable of holding 15,000 gallons. At the same time, the *Wanderer's* luxurious furnishings were retained and, flying the flag of the New York Yacht Club, she was to the casual eye still a rich man's plaything.

On 3 July 1858, with Captain Semmes in command and several passengers on board, including William Corrie, the *Wanderer* sailed to Trinidad, where she was treated with due respect by the British authorities. She left Port of Spain on 27 July, her destination being declared as St. Helena. Once out of sight of the land, she set course for the River Congo, where she arrived on 16 September.

The River Congo was at that time the last major centre for the slave trade remaining on the west coast of Africa. The 20-mile-wide mouth of the Congo, studded with numerous islands, provided excellent cover for slavers hiding from the attentions of the anti-slavery cruisers. Anchored in the lee of a wooded island, a slave-runner with her cargo already on board needed only to wait for a dark night and then shoot out on the fast-flowing Congo current, which would carry her 60 miles out to sea before the dawn came.

As the *Wanderer's* cargo of slaves was not yet ready for shipment, Semmes anchored her just inside the mouth of the river, making no attempt to hide from the prying eyes of the African Squadron. He was not surprised when a few days later HMS *Medusa*, passing by on patrol, came in to investigate. The *Medusa*, a wooden paddle steamer of 889 tons, was under the command of Commander William Bowden, an officer very experienced in the ways of the slavers. William Corrie, however, who was effectively in command of the *Wanderer*, decided to pre-empt the inevitable visit of a boarding party by inviting Commander Bowden and his officers to dinner on board the yacht. This was a rare relief from the boredom of the anti-slavery patrol, and Bowden, impressed by the New York Yacht Club pennant the *Wanderer* was still flying, was delighted to accept the invitation.

Bowden was even more impressed when he saw the sumptuous furnishings aboard the *Wanderer*. The wine flowed, and during the course of an excellent dinner Corrie brazenly invited Bowden to inspect his ship, just to reassure himself that the *Wanderer* was not a slaver. Bowden laughingly declined, certain in his mind that no one guilty of carrying slaves would ever willingly throw open his ship to inspection by the Royal Navy.

When Commander Bowden and his officers had disembarked, and the *Medusa* had made her way back out to sea, the *Wanderer* moved up river to a pre-arranged rendezvous, and there took on 500 slaves, 'prime Negroes between the ages of thirteen and eighteen.' She sailed from the Congo on 18 October, only to find that the *Medusa* was still outside. The *Medusa*'s log shows that some of her officers again boarded the *Wanderer*, but they obviously saw nothing to lead them to suspect that the yacht had 500 slaves battened down in her hold.

The *Wanderer* met adverse winds in the Atlantic, and six weeks went by before she arrived off the coast of Georgia. Not surprisingly, eighty of her slaves had died on passage; the rest were secretly landed on Jekyll Island, near the port of Brunswick, on 28 November. They were then smuggled up river to Charles Lamar's plantation. Unfortunately for Lamar, word of the arrival of the slaves reached the ears of the authorities, and an arrest warrant was nailed to the *Wanderer*'s mast. Lamar was arrested and charged with slave trading, but the great plantations of the Southern States were totally dependent on slave labour, and he was acquitted by a sympathetic court. The *Wanderer* was sold at a public auction, which Charles Lamar attended. It was denied that the auction was rigged, but by some means or other Lamar managed to buy back his own ship at a quarter of her real value. The slaves who survived the *Wanderer*'s Atlantic crossing were also sold, most probably ending up on Lamar's plantation, or those of his many friends. However, Captain William Corrie obviously did not have influential friends at court. He was found guilty of slave trading, and spent some time in prison. He was also expelled from the New York Yacht Club.

Word of the *Wanderer*'s ability to elude the anti-slaving patrols had spread in American shipping circles, and Lamar was able to sell her on at a handsome profit. Her new owner appointed

Captain D.S Martin to command, and immediately sent her off on a voyage to Dahomey to pick up slaves. It seems that although Martin was quite happy engage in the slave trade, his crew were not. They mutinied when they were within sight of the Canary Islands, put Captain Martin into a small boat to go his own way, and took the *Wanderer* back to Boston, where she was handed over to the authorities again.

The *Wanderer* was in the news again two years later. A week before the outbreak of war between the North and the Southern States, which was to end in the abolition of slavery in the United States, she arrived in Key West, Florida. There she was caught up in the fighting and was confiscated by Union forces. Ironically, she ended her days as a dispatch boat for the Union's East Gulf Blockading Squadron.

Thanks to the dedication of the Royal Navy's African Squadron, the steady flow of slaves across the Atlantic from West Africa had all but dried up. But that still left the internal slavery – African enslaving African – which would continue to flourish for many years to come. An expedition sent to Benin in 1897 found the streets of the city 'strewn with crucified and decapitated corpses,' slaves sacrificed to placate pagan gods. This was common practice in the area.

In the Moslem north of Nigeria, slave hunting was a popular sport of the rulers. Periodically, their cavalry would sweep southwards across the Niger or eastwards into the Cameroons to collect fresh slaves. Questioned by a British official as to the need for this, the Emir of Kontagora replied, 'Can you stop a cat from mousing?' He went on, 'When I die, I shall be found with a slave in my mouth.' Putting a stop to such misery inflicted by brother on brother would prove to be almost impossible.

Chapter Thirteen

The Sultan's Domain

Commander John Lodwick Royal Navy

*In Memory of John Lodwick, Esquire, Commander R.N.
Eldest son of John Lodwick, Esqre of Rochford Hall, and
Ann, his wife. He served his country with distinction, in every
quarter of the world, for a period of 20 years and was
promoted for his gallantry in an encounter with a slave ship,
on the 12th January 1845, when he was dangerously
wounded. Shortly afterwards he fell victim to the pestilential
fever of the Coast of Africa and died May 13th 1845, aged 35
years. This tablet was erected by a few of his friends, to mark
their admiration and respect for his gallant and truly
estimable character.*

Memorial at St. Andrew's Church, Rochford, Essex

Operating in parallel with the West African slave trade, a similar
trade, only of much earlier origin, flourished on the far side of the
African continent. There was, however, a fundamental difference
in the East African trade, in that it was almost exclusively in the
hands of the Arabs, who had been involved in the exploitation of
Africans for nearly 2,000 years. Their expertise in catching and
transporting slaves was such that the recently arrived Europeans
appeared rank amateurs by comparison.

Making use of the seasonal winds of the Indian Ocean
monsoon, the first Arab traders are believed to have reached East
Africa from the Arabian Peninsula sometime in the first millenni-
um BC. Greek writings dated as early as the 1st century AD spoke
of the northern part of the coast of East Africa as being settled by

the Arabs, who were noted for their export of slaves. The first indication that a substantial trade in slaves was being carried on came some 600 years later, when it was recorded that large numbers of African slaves were being transported to work on plantations in Mesopotamia, the area today known as Iraq. There is also evidence that for many centuries the caravans of Arab traders were journeying as far south as Lake Chad in search of black slaves for the palaces and households of their kingdoms on the southern shores of the Mediterranean. The Arab geographer Al Yaqubi remarked, 'I have been informed that the kings of the blacks sell their own people without justification or in consequence of war.' As Sharia Law sanctioned slavery, and even laid down the rules to be adhered to when taking slaves, to the Arabs the trade was eminently justified. The traders certainly had little difficulty in making up their coffles, as long before they arrived on the scene slavery had been an accepted part of everyday life in these isolated corners of Africa. When an Arab caravan appeared, the local chieftains were only too eager to make war on their neighbours. The 'prisoners of war' taken, including women and children, were sold to the traders from the north, more often than not for a handful of worthless trinkets. If the Arabs were unable to trade for slaves, they were not above carrying out their own raids to gather in unsuspecting Africans, and they were well enough armed to be able do this.

The early Arab slave traders were not dealing in great numbers. The slaves, valuable though they might be, were really only an additional commodity to add to the ivory, gold and spices, which were the primary reasons for the caravans making the long journey into the African interior. It was not until the late 17th century, when the date plantations of Oman began to expand, that the Arab slave trade increased dramatically. Then the sugar planters in the French colonies on the islands to the east of Madagascar suddenly found themselves facing an acute shortage of labour. Slave markets were set up on Zanzibar and neighbouring Pemba, which by the 1840s were handling up to 20,000 slaves annually. The slave trade and the large-scale cultivation of cloves on the island by slave labour became so lucrative that the Sultan of Oman, Sheikh Seyyid Said, moved his court 2000 miles south to Zanzibar.

In 1841 Captain Hamerton took up residence as the British Consul in Zanzibar, and was encouraged by the Foreign Office to bring pressure to bear on the Sultan to put an end to the Arab slave trade in East Africa. Sultan Said, whose annual revenue from the trade was in the region of £20,000, was reluctant to kill his golden goose, but in 1845, he eventually concluded a treaty with Hamerton prohibiting the export of slaves from the African mainland. This treaty permitted slaves to be brought from the mainland to Zanzibar Island, ostensibly to work in the clove plantations; but in reality Zanzibar became a staging post for the export of slaves, mainly to the Persian Gulf. Every year, in December, fleets of dhows, manned by the piratical Suri tribesmen from South Arabia, came southwards on the wings of the north-east monsoon, returning with their cargoes of slaves in April, when the monsoon blew the other way.

The Suri dhows were large craft up to 100 tons, with two masts, and manned by a crew of about forty. They were armed with anti-quated 3-pounder carronades, and their crews carried flintlock muskets and heavy cutlasses, which they used to great effect when threatened. Built to a centuries old design, and with large lateen sails, the dhows were capable of phenomenal speeds when running before the winds of the monsoons. From the point of view of the unfortunate slaves, however, the dhow was far from being the ideal means of transport, even on short voyages. Captain Fairfax Moresby, the Senior British Officer on Mauritius, wrote regarding the shipment of slaves from the mainland to Zanzibar:

> In these vessels temporary platforms of bamboos are erected, leaving a narrow passage in the centre. The Negroes are then stowed, in the literal sense of the word, in bulk, the first along the floor of the vessel, two adults side by side, with a boy or girl resting between them or on them, until the tier is complete. Over them the first platform is laid, supported an inch or two clear of their bodies, when a second tier is stowed, and so on until they reach above the gunwale of the vessel. The voyage, they expect, will not exceed 24 or 48 hours; but it often happens that a calm or unexpected land breeze delays their progress. In this case a few hours are sufficient to decide

the fate of the cargo. Those of the lower portion of the cargo that die cannot be removed. They remain until the upper part are dead and thrown over. And from a cargo of 200 to 400 stowed in this way, it has been known that not a dozen at the expiration of ten days have reached Zanzibar.

Colonel Christopher Rigby, an officer in the Indian Army, was appointed British Consul in Zanzibar in 1858, and was horrified by the trade his predecessor had apparently allowed to flourish in the island. He wrote:

It is impossible to conceive a more revolting sight than the landing of slaves coming from Kilwa. They are brought in open boats, packed so closely (and in a state of complete nudity) that they are exposed day and night to sun, wind and rain, with only sufficient grain to keep them from starvation. If the boats meet with contrary winds, they generally run short of water, and thirst is added to the other miseries which those poor creatures endure. On arriving at Zanzibar, they are frequently unable to stand; some drop dead in the customs house and in the streets, and others who are not likely to recover are left on board to die, in order that the master may avoid paying the duty which is levied on those landed. After being brought on shore the slaves are kept some time in the dealer's houses until they gain flesh and strength, when they are sold at auction in the slave market. The Arab regards the slaves as cattle; not the slightest attention is paid to their sufferings; they are too cheap and numerous to be cared for. This year slaves have been sold in the interior for half a dollar a head, and five slaves given in exchange for a cow or bullock.

The trading in slaves in the streets of Zanzibar was quite blatant. Captain George Sulivan, on a visit to the port with HMS *Daphne*, was horrified at what he saw:

Passing the Sultan's palace, the good-looking exteriors of the houses of the 'well to do' Arab population, and through the filthy streets, we emerge by a narrow lane into a small square – large for Zanzibar. Here the first thing that meets the eye is a number of slaves arranged in a semicircle, with their faces towards us and the centre of the square. Most of them are standing up, but some are sitting on the ground; some of them, in fact, utterly incapable of standing upon their feet, miserable, emaciated skeletons, on whom disease, and perhaps starvation, has placed its fatal mark. If those who are sitting down had evinced half the stubbornness on the mainland that they do here, they would have been knocked on the head and left a prey to the wild beasts; but there is a limit to such treatment in Zanzibar, on account of the presence of the Europeans...In another portion of the square are a number of women, forming several semicircles; their bodies are painted, and their figures exposed to the examination of throngs of Arabs, and subject to inexpressible indignities by the brutal dealers. On entering the market on one occasion we saw several Arab slavedealers around these poor creatures; they were in treaty for the purchase of three or four women, who had been made to take off the only rag of a garment which they wore. On catching sight of English faces there was a commotion amongst the Arabs, and the women were hurried off round a corner out of sight...

The British East African Squadron, which waged a continuous and largely thankless fight against the slaving dhows, rarely consisted of more than three ships, seven at the most. This tiny force was expected to keep watch over the coastline of East Africa, the Mozambique Channel, the islands to the east, and as far north as the coast of Baluchistan in the Arabian Sea. The ships were all steamers, and as such had the capacity to overhaul the fast Arab dhows, but when under steam they burned 26 tons of coal a day, and as their bunkers held only 76 tons, the coal had to be used sparingly. Furthermore, coal in Zanzibar cost £8 a ton, around thirty times as much as in home waters, and any commander who wasted coal on a futile chase was soon called to account by the Admiralty. Consequently, the squadron's ships were for the most part under sail, and boilers were fired up only when a good capture was certain.

Captain John Wilson, commanding the steam sloop HMS *Gorgon*, wrote:

It is difficult to imagine the real horrors of this dhow traffic, especially with the northerners. They have a voyage of nearly 1,500 miles from Zanzibar to the Persian Gulf, and during the whole time the slaves are exposed to the weather quite naked, and are very badly fed, their daily rations being just sufficient to keep life and soul together, and sometimes not even that. From daylight until evening the wretched slaves sit under the rays of a tropical sun half famished. About sunset a meal is served out to them. From a mess of burnt boiled millet seed a platterful is given to a crowd of 30...After this a drink of water is allowed; then they are left to hunger and thirst, cold and heat, cramp and stench for the next 24 hours...Generally speaking, about one half of the cargo reaches its destination alive, the mortality being caused by starvation and disease, and this when the dhow is sailing along quietly enough with no cruisers in sight. When chased, the poor slaves are very often murdered and thrown overboard...

When Commander Radulphus Oldfield brought the steam sloop *Lyra* into Zanzibar harbour towards the end of February 1861, he found the port in a state of armed chaos. A large number of Arab dhows, manned by Suris, had recently arrived in the harbour, and having purchased slaves from the market, they were about to return north on the first of the south-west monsoon winds. But before sailing, the Suris had gone on the rampage through the town, putting to the sword any locals foolish enough to oppose them. The US consulate had already been attacked, and Sultan Seyed Burgash-bin-Said, successor to Sheikh Seyyid Said, had barricaded himself in his palace. Oldfield had no authority to interfere, and after consulting with Colonel Rigby, decided to set off in pursuit of another fleet of dhows, which had just sailed carrying an estimated 2000 slaves. On the high seas Oldfield faced no restrictions on his authority.

Using engine and sails, *Lyra* caught up with the Arab dhows two days out of Zanzibar. Oldfield sent away his whaleboat, and in a running battle the boat captured a dhow with 99 slaves on board. Over the course of the next twenty-four hours, *Lyra*'s boats took three more dhows with a total of 150 slaves. Having made his mark on the slavers, Oldfield then returned to Zanzibar, arriving back on 31 March.

The situation in Zanzibar had changed little while *Lyra* was away. There were still a number of Suri dhows in port, and their crews continued to wreak havoc ashore, but now their anger had been turned against the white men. In consultation with Colonel Rigby, Commander Oldfield decided to remain in port, hoping that the *Lyra*'s presence would act as a deterrent to the rioters. And now, with the connivance of Rigby and the Sultan, Oldfield began systematically boarding and searching those dhows in port. Over the next four days, *Lyra*'s boats patrolled the harbour and boarded a number of dhows suspected of slaving. Only one dhow was found with slaves on board, ninety-five in all, and this was taken by force. Several other dhows were boarded in the face of stiff resistance, resulting in three of *Lyra*'s seamen being injured. One of her boats was lost.

As the rioting continued unabated, Zanzibar descended into a state of complete anarchy, the only law and order in the port being in the hands of HMS *Lyra* and her armed seamen. This being so, Oldfield and Rigby persuaded the Sultan to agree to clearing all the Suri dhows out of the harbour. Word was sent to the dhows that they had three days grace in which to load any cargo other than slaves, before sailing out of the port, and then only after being searched by the Royal Navy. Any dhows remaining in port on expiry of the 72 hours would be seized and burned.

Characteristically, the Suris ignored Oldfield's proclamation and, in fact, when the commander was visiting his guard boats his gig was attacked by two dhows. Although Oldfield was in a 16ft boat with fewer than a dozen armed men, he fought back, boarding and capturing one of the dhows. The other dhow got away, but two of its crew were killed. Oldfield's gig was damaged by Arab gunfire, but only one seaman was injured.

That night, under the cover of a diversion which drew the guard boats away from the harbour entrance, eleven dhows managed to escape with slaves on board. Another ultimatum was issued to the remaining dhows, and by late afternoon the next day only five were remaining in port. These were seized and burnt on Oldfield's orders.

The drastic action taken by Commander Oldfield and Consul Rigby, not always with the Sultan's blessing, resulted in the destruction of sixteen Arab dhows and the release of some 250 slaves. For a while, at least, Zanzibar was free of these odious craft and their troublesome crews. But the supply of slaves on mainland Africa being inexhaustible, and the demand from the north as great as ever, Zanzibar's period of grace was short.

Under the terms of the Hamerton Treaty, it was still legal to import slaves to work in the island's clove plantations, an industry which required around 1,700 slaves annually. However, even the most conservative of estimates reported the number of slaves being landed in Zanzibar every year as between 20,000 and 60,000. As there was no visible increase in the number of Africans working in the clove fields, it followed that the Suri dhows were as active as ever. Nor was there any let-up in the ferocity of the resistance met with by the men of the East African Squadron, whose bravery in the face of tremendous odds was unquestionable. A typical example was the treatment of one of HMS *Lyra*'s boats' crews in 1864.

Lyra was passing the entrance to the Mogincual River, 50 miles south of the Portuguese fort at Mozambique, when a suspicious dhow was seen anchored inside the bar. A cutter manned by Lieutenant Reed and a crew of six was sent in to investigate, while *Lyra* continued on up the coast. Unfortunately, while attempting to cross the bar, the cutter got into difficulties in the heavy surf and was sunk. Reed and his men managed to swim ashore, but their arms had gone down with their boat.

When the seven men settled down on the beach to await rescue by their ship they were attacked by a large crowd of armed Arabs. Unable to defend themselves, the British party fled into the bush, where two of their number were killed by the Arabs, and Lieutenant Reed and one other were taken prisoner. The two men were later released by the intervention of a friendly Arab chief, who was no doubt influenced by the reappearance off the river of HMS *Lyra*.

One dhow captured by *Lyra* on this occasion was bound from Kilwa to Zanzibar, and when boarded was found to be carrying 100 young girls destined for the harems of Arabia. The girls, who were without food and water, were packed so tightly together that they were only just able to breathe, and the stench was enough to make even the hardened seamen vomit. Had the dhow been becalmed for any length of time, it is probable that few of the girls would have survived.

On 12 October 1867 HMS *Daphne* arrived in Zanzibar. She was the latest addition to the African Squadron, having been commissioned only four months earlier at Plymouth. Commanded by Commander George Sulivan, *Daphne* was a 1640-ton screw steamer, armed with four guns and carrying a crew of 150. Sulivan reported on arrival, 'We found the harbour literally crowded with dhows of every kind, and among them several full of slaves…'

Not having the authority to board dhows in the harbour, Sulivan left port on the afternoon of the 21st, having let it be known that his ship was bound for Bombay. Once out of sight of Zanzibar, *Daphne* altered course to close the African coast, and then sailed north for 500 miles. On the evening of the 24th Sulivan came to an anchor in a bay off the old walled town of Brava on the coast of Somalia, a favourite stopping off place for the northbound dhows. He was prepared to wait for the Suris to come to him.

Sulivan did not have long to wait; the first dhow made an appearance on the afternoon of the 25th. *Daphne* immediately weighed anchor, and after a short chase stopped and boarded the dhow. Unfortunately for Commander Sulivan, this was one dhow he should have allowed to pass. She was from Zanzibar all right, but her only passengers were a sister of the Sultan and her fifteen domestic slaves. Not wishing to cause a diplomatic incident, Sulivan allowed the dhow to go on its way.

The first opportunity for Commander Sulivan to really exercise his authority came three days later, when another dhow appeared from the south. As before, *Daphne* steamed to intercept, but on seeing the British ship approaching, the dhow put her helm up and steered for the shore. Whether by design or accident, she ploughed through the breakers and ended up on the beach a total wreck.

Unable to take the *Daphne* closer to the shore, Sulivan watched in horror as a horde of black slaves poured out of the wreck and struggled through the raging surf to the shore, many appearing to drown on the way. Although the seas breaking on the sand bar fronting the beach were awesome – Sulivan remarked, 'I never saw worse looking breakers, not even at Buffalo Mouth or Algoa Bay' – a boat was lowered, and set off for the beach. Sulivan, always willing to take the same risks as his men, went with the boat.

As the boat approached the line of foaming breakers the noise of the tumbling seas was like rolling thunder, and Sulivan began to have second thoughts about attempting to land. His mind was made up for him when the boat was lifted on the back of a huge groundswell and surged forward. Then they were in the surf, and seas were sweeping the boat from end to end, threatening to tear the oarsmen from the thwarts. It was only the frantic efforts of Sulivan and Midshipman Breen, who were handling the tiller yokes, that the boat did not broach to and spill them all into the surf. Suddenly they were through the maelstrom and into comparatively calm water. Glancing astern, Sulivan wondered how on earth they would ever get out again.

When they ran the boat up on the sand the beach was empty; only the line of bodies floating face down in the shallow water was evidence of the tragedy that they had so recently seen acted out. The other slaves, the lucky ones, had disappeared into the bush. Of their captors there was no sign. A search of the sand dunes backing the beach revealed only seven terrified African children who had been left behind. When questioned the youngsters said that the dhow had been crammed with slaves, and when the *Daphne* was sighted the Arabs sent them into a panic by telling them the white men had come to eat them.

With darkness not far off, and reluctant to tackle the surf in the half-light, Sulivan had decided to spend the night on the beach, when an angry crowd of about twenty Somalis appeared out of the bush brandishing spears and muskets. As they advanced on the little party, Sulivan fired a warning shot over their heads, and to his great relief the Somalis retreated in confusion. Before they recovered their wits, he had bundled the children into the boat and cast off. Once out of range of the Somali muskets, Sulivan waited until there was a slight lull in the swell before tackling the breakers. Then, with the oarsmen pulling for their lives, and the terrified African children clinging to the bottom boards, he put the boat to the surf and broke out into the open sea.

Over the next six days, *Daphne* was kept busy as a steady

stream of northbound dhows sailed past her anchorage. At one time, all her five boats, two cutters, a gig, a whaler and a dinghy, were engaged in chasing and boarding dhows. Of one of the dhows captured Sulivan wrote:

> On the morning of the 1st November, we observed the cutter, under charge of Mr. Henn, chasing a dhow outside her, which, on seeing us, lowered her sail, and a few minutes after she was brought alongside, with 156 slaves in her, forty-eight men, fifty-three women, and fifty-five children. The deplorable condition of some of these poor wretches, crammed into a small dhow, surpasses all description; on the bottom of the dhow was a pile of stones as ballast, and on these stones, without even a mat, were twenty-three women huddled together – one or two with infants in their arms – these women were literally doubled up, there being no room to sit erect; on a bamboo deck, about three feet above the keel, were forty-eight men, crowded together in the same way, and on another deck above this were fifty-three children. Some of the slaves were in the last stages of starvation and dysentery. On getting the vessel alongside and clearing her out, a woman came up, having an infant about a month or six weeks old in her arms, with one side of its forehead crushed in. On asking how it was done, she told us that just before our boat came alongside the dhow, the child began to cry, and one of the Arabs, fearing the English would hear it, took up a stone, and struck it. A few hours after this the poor thing died, and the woman was too weak and ill to be able to point out the monster who had done it, from amongst the ten or dozen Arabs on board.

The *Daphne* was by this time running short of coal and when, on 4 November, the gun vessel HMS *Star* appeared, Sulivan directed her commander to remain in the area while he went in search of bunkers. *Daphne* now had 322 slaves on board, rescued from the fifteen dhows she had stopped in the eleven days she had been off Brava, and Sulivan decided to go north to Aden to land them. At the same time, he hoped to replenish his bunkers.

Daphne headed north under sail only, but when she was 400 miles south of Cape Guardafui, at the entrance to the Gulf of

Aden, she ran into an area of calms. With only 10 tons of coal remaining on board, Sulivan could not afford to use his engine, and the sloop drifted, her sails hanging limp, and the current carrying her south at the rate of 24 miles a day. Having an extra 322 souls on board, all requiring food and water, of which he had precious little, Sulivan was in serious trouble. He tried to sail south-east to the Seychelles, where he knew there was a supply of coal, but there was not enough wind. By 18 November *Daphne* had drifted so far south that there was no feasible alternative but to return to Zanzibar. She reached there three weeks after parting company with the *Star*, having just enough coal left to get her into the harbour.

When, in March 1872, Rear-Admiral Arthur Cumming was appointed Commander-in Chief East Indies, he had nine ships on station. Of these, six were fully employed in Indian waters, leaving only two ships to patrol the whole coast of Africa from Cape Guardafui in the north to the southern end of the Mozambique Channel. This was the East African Squadron of 1872. Little wonder that when Admiral Cumming reported to the Admiralty at the end of the year, he could offer little in the way of progress in the fight against the slave trade. In the nine months he had been commanding the station the two-ship East African Squadron had captured only six dhows and released 251 slaves; and this against the background of a total of 15,129 slaves being landed in Zanzibar from 1 May to 31 December of that year, most of whom were then re-exported. One of the slaving dhows was stopped by HMS *Vulture* as far north as Ras-Al-Had in the Gulf of Oman. An account of this capture was published in the *Times of India* in October 1872:

> The number of slaves it was impossible at the time to estimate. So crowded on deck, and in the hold below was the dhow, that it seemed, but for the aspect of misery, a very nest of ants. The hold, from which an intolerable stench proceeded, was several inches deep in the foulest bilge water and refuse. Down below, there were numbers of children and wretched beings in the most loathsome stages of smallpox and scrofula of every description. A more disgusting and degrading spectacle of humanity could hardly be seen, whilst the

foulness of the dhow was such that the sailors could hardly endure it. When the slaves were transferred to the *Vulture*, the poor wretched creatures were so dreadfully emaciated and weak, that many had to be carried on board, and lifted for every movement. How it was that so many had survived such hardships was a source of wonder to all that belonged to the *Vulture*.

The dhow was taken to Bombay, where it was established that the slaves originally numbered an astonishing 1,691. Of these, fifteen had died on the passage north, and surgeons discovered that there were no fewer than thirty-five cases of smallpox amongst those remaining. Later it was learned that when smallpox was first discovered on board, the thirty-six heavily armed Arabs comprising the crew of the dhow began throwing overboard those infected. In all, forty slaves had suffered this cruel death before HMS *Vulture* came on the scene.

Although Admiral Cumming had so few ships at his disposal, their successes were considerable, prompting the Admiral to offer advice to London on the disposal of their spoils. He wrote, 'I would suggest that, for the future, at all events for some time to come, all liberated slaves should be sent to the Seychelles Islands; labour is much wanted there, and the resources of the islands are capable of development; but the system of supervision and seeing that the labourers are properly allotted, looked after, and cared for, is open to much improvement. There are several public works, such as a pier, roads across to the Island of Mahé, &c., in progress, but which get on slowly for want of labour.'

Chapter Fourteen

The Last of the Trade

Benjamin Stone A.B.

Sacred to the memory of Benjamin Stone, A.B. HMS
Turquoise, who died from the effects of wounds received
during an engagement with a slave dhow off Fundo Gap 11
June 1887, age 20 years.

O Comrades stay as you pass by as you are now so once was
I; as I am now you must be prepared for death to follow me.

Memorial on Funzi Island, Tanzania

In April 1872 Zanzibar was hit by a storm of catastrophic
intensity that had a profound and lasting effect on the economy
of the island.

On the afternoon of 15 April a south-westerly gale – a rare
enough occurrence in these waters – which had been blowing
since early morning, suddenly developed into a full cyclone with
winds up to 100 knots, accompanied by torrential rains. The
narrow streets of the port became raging torrents carrying all
before them, flimsy native huts were blown away, and swathes of
trees uprooted.

Zanzibar's Arab landowners suffered the heaviest loss. Two
thirds of their clove and coconut plantations had been destroyed,
and as new trees planted would not bear fruit for many years, the
loss was one from which they would probably never recover. In
the harbour 150 dhows, many of them potential slave carriers,
were sunk or thrown ashore, while the small navy, founded and
built up by Sultan Seyyid Said, had lost its flagship, and three
other ships were badly damaged. In the space of a few hours the
face of Zanzibar had been completely changed.

171

The April cyclone did not affect the work of the African Squadron, which continued to record a steady catalogue of successes against the slave traders. A year later, on 31 May 1873, Dr John Kirk, the British Political Agent at Zanzibar, was able to report to London that the slave traffic through the island had all but dried up. He wrote:

So thoroughly indeed have the steps taken achieved the object aimed at, that whereas in former years over 4000 slaves have usually been imported here by the end of May, this season only two small cargoes have been entered at the Custom-house – one with nineteen and the other with two slaves on board...The Sultan's Custom-house has in fact only realized in slave duties during the month, 116 dollars, against a sum of 8,290 dollars drawn from the same source as duties for 4,145 slaves imported during the same month of 1872.

The Senior Naval Officer, Captain Malcolm, of the *Briton*, has by a well-planned disposition of every available boat, and the skilful management of the slender means at his disposal, paralysed the Arabs, who fear at every town the sudden appearance either of the ships or one of their boats – to such an extent, indeed, that the weakness of the fleet is [a] matter of public disbelief.

Now that his revenue from the trade was insignificant and under increasing pressure from the British government, in June 1873 the Sultan of Zanzibar finally agreed to sign a treaty outlawing the slave trade in his territories. The Treaty for the Suppression of the Slave Trade stated that:

The provisions of the existing Treaties having proved ineffectual for preventing the export of slaves from the territories of the Sultan of Zanzibar in Africa, Her Majesty the Queen and His Highness the Sultan above named agree that from this date the export of slaves from the coast of mainland Africa, whether destined for transport from one part of the Sultan's dominions to another or for conveyance to foreign parts, shall entirely cease. And his Highness the Sultan binds himself, to the best of his ability, to make an effectual arrangement throughout his dominions to prevent and abolish the same.

172

And any vessel engaged in the transport or conveyance of slaves, after this date, shall be liable to seizure and condemnation by all such naval or other officers or agents, and such Courts, as may be authorized for that purpose on the part of her Majesty.

In addition, Sultan bin-Said agreed to close all the slave markets on Zanzibar, thereby depriving himself of what had once been a very handsome income, reputed to be in the region of £20,000 a year. However, he had little or no authority over the Suri Arabs, who were the main traffickers. But at least his compliance gave legitimacy to the work of the African Squadron, which by then had been considerably reinforced. The two ships already on station, the steam sloops *Briton* and *Daphne*, had been joined by the 4th rate screw frigate *Glasgow* and the steam sloops *Wolverene*, *Vulture*, *Nimble*, *Magpie* and *Shearwater*. This gave Rear-Admiral Cumming a very considerable fleet with which to enforce the treaty, albeit only for as long as the Admiralty thought necessary.

A year later, in July 1874, Admiral Cumming reported:

During the slave-running season of March, April and May, a most careful blockade of the coast of Africa, to the northward of Zanzibar, has been made by the *Briton*, *Daphne*, and *Vulture*, assisted by their boats, and during the latter part of the season I stationed the *Philomel* and *Rifleman* on the north-west coast of Arabia, to search any dhows which might have escaped the vigilance of the ships in the south. But not one illegal trader has been found, though a great number of dhows have been boarded, and from the reports I have received I learn that not the slightest sign of any attempt to convey slaves to the north was found, and I therefore consider that the effect of the late Treaty, as far as sea traffic in slaves is concerned, is most satisfactory.

It did now seem that at last the battle against the East African slave trade had been won. However, the Arabs were not about to give up their ancient traffic without a fight. Accepting that the Royal Navy had driven their dhows off the sea, they simply reverted to the overland route. They began to harvest their slaves

173

deep in Central Africa, along the banks of the River Congo, and march them overland through Kenya, Tanganyika and Somaliland to the Gulf of Aden. The Arab caravans or coffles usually consisted of a hundred or more slaves, shackled together and further hampered by being made to carry heavy loads of ivory or stores. Their Arab masters made liberal use of the whip to drive them on, the coffle being expected to make up to 20 miles in a day, often through very hostile territory. Many of the captives died on the way to the coast, their bodies being left to the mercy of the wild beasts of the forests. Those who survived the 2000-mile trek were herded aboard dhows anchored off the coast to make the crossing to the Arabian Peninsula.

Some dhows did manage to evade the net spread by the African Squadron by sailing from ports in the south and giving Zanzibar a wide berth. One who survived such a voyage was Petro Kilekwa, captured by an Arab raiding party in Tanganyika. Along with several hundred other captives, he was taken to the coast near Mikindani, then marched north for three days to Kilwa. There they were put aboard a dhow bound for Muscat, a daunting passage of over 2,500 miles. Kilekwa later described his journey:

> On the third evening we saw a big dhow and that same night we went on board and all the slaves were placed on the lower deck. We travelled all night and in the morning we found we were in the midst of the sea and out of sight of land. We went on thus for many days over the sea. At first we had food twice a day, in the morning and in the evening. The men had two platefuls and the women two and for our relish we often had fish, for our masters the Arabs caught a large number of fish with hooks and line. But because the journey was so long the food began to run short and so we were hungry, and also water was short and they began to mix it with salt water.

Most of the slaves had had little or no contact with Europeans, and their innocence was cruelly exploited by their Arab captors, who convinced them they would be eaten if they fell into the hands of the white man. When the dhow was intercepted by a British naval ship in the Gulf of Oman the Africans were terrified. Petro Kilekwa later testified:

174

We were told, 'Europeans are coming! They have sighted us. Their boat is a long way off. They do not want us Arabs, certainly not! But they are after you slaves and they will eat you and they will grind your bones and make sweetmeats of them. Europeans are much whiter than we Arabs are – hide yourselves!'

Kilekwa described what transpired when the dhow was boarded by the Royal Navy:

When we saw the face of the European we were terrified. We were quite certain that Europeans eat people but the European said to the black man: 'Tell them not to be afraid but let them rejoice,' and the European began to smile and to laugh. And the sailor and the black man told the other Europeans who were on the boat, 'There are slaves here, ever so many of them.'

In the course of his travels on the continent, the missionary and explorer David Livingstone saw at first hand the treatment of the Africans by the Arab slave traders. On 15 July 1871 he was seated in the shade in the marketplace of the village of Nyangwe, on the Lualaba River, when a party of Arab traders arrived. There was an argument with the locals, which led to the Arabs opening fire on the crowd. The sound of gunfire brought more Arabs, who joined in the slaughter. Livingstone wrote in his diary: 'Men opened fire on the mass of people near the upper end of the marketplace, and volleys were discharged from a party down near the creek on the panic-stricken women who dashed at the canoes. These, some 50 or more, were jammed in the creek and the men forgot their paddles in the terror that seized all.'

The Arabs then lined the riverbank and calmly began firing on the canoes. Those who leapt from their canoes and began swimming were picked off in the water. Livingstone, powerless to intervene, and obviously distraught at the terrible scene he was witnessing, confided to his diary: 'As I write I hear the loud wails on the left bank over those who are slain, ignorant of their many friends who are now in the depths of the Lualaba. Oh, let Thy kingdom come!'

The most notorious of the slave traders operating in the upper

175

reaches of the Congo was Tippoo Tib, who was part Arab and part African. Born in Zanzibar of a half Arab, half Negro father and a Negro mother, Tippoo Tib had the physique of his mother's race and the guile of his Arab grandfather. He became a ruthless trader, ranging far inland with an armed band of several hundred men. Anything he was unable to barter for, including slaves, he took by force of arms. He marched caravans of slaves across Africa, carrying gold and ivory on their heads, firstly to Mozambique for shipment to Zanzibar, and when that outlet was closed, north to the land of the Somalis.

Figures received by Rear-Admiral Cumming from a reliable source showed that in the first six months of 1874 nearly 12,000 slaves had been taken north by the overland route. It was also reported that few of these slaves had reached Arabia, their primary destination in past years. The Arab slave traders had found other markets for their wares, presumably in Somaliland, where there was a great demand for labour following the occupation of the territory by the Egyptians.

Cummings had also received intelligence that slaves were being shipped to Madagascar from the coast of Mozambique, the intention being to re-export them by dhow to the Persian Gulf from the northern end of the island. The prediction that the treaty of 1873 had signed the death warrant of the East African slave trade was proving premature. Zanzibar's principal slave market was closed, its shame hidden by the building of a Christian cathedral on the site, but still a trickle of slaves found its way across the narrow strip of water separating the island from the mainland. And still the Suri dhows came to anchor in the harbour, feigning respectability by loading cargoes of spices and local produce, but continuing to smuggle slaves out whenever they were available.

George Sulivan, lately promoted to captain, returned to Zanzibar in April 1874 in command of HMS *London*. The 4375-ton *London*, launched in 1840, was a wooden two-decker, a ship of the line mounting 90 guns and manned by a complement of 850. In 1858 she had been converted to steam, but five years later was taken out of service and laid up in Plymouth until such time as some useful employment could be found for her. This came in 1874, when it was decided to send her to Zanzibar as headquarters and depot ship for the East African Squadron.

On arrival in Zanzibar, the *London*'s engine was removed, and she was permanently anchored in the harbour as mother ship to a flotilla of smaller slaver-hunting craft. She was commissioned as such in 1878, and equipped with five 40ft sailing cutters, each mounting a 7-pounder muzzle loader, a 42ft schooner-rigged launch, a steam pinnace and a small steam cutter. Each boat was manned by a midshipman or a lieutenant, a coxswain, an interpreter, and eight men. The boats were kept at five minutes readiness, and were stocked with food and water sufficient for them to stay at sea for a month at a time. *London*'s slave hunters soon became the scourge of the Indian Ocean. In their first two years on operations they captured and destroyed thirty-nine dhows totalling nearly 2,500 tons, and liberated over 500 slaves.

The years, teredo worm and the unrelenting rays of the tropical sun took their toll of *London*, and when Captain Charles Brownrigg took command in June 1880, her wooden hull was rotten, her upper masts gone, and what remained of her rigging was unsafe. Below decks she was infested with rats and cockroaches, and at any one time sixty or seventy of her complement were to be found in the sick bay.

Charles Brownrigg was a naval officer of considerable experience, having served with distinction in many oceans and wars. He was also fiercely unconventional, always ready to turn a Nelsonian blind eye when needed, and possessed a good sense of humour. But perhaps his outstanding qualities were the ability to put himself on the same level as those under him and his willingness to take the same risks. It was the latter that cost him his life.

On the morning of 27 November 1881 Captain Brownrigg left the *London* in the steam pinnace, crewed by Leading Seaman Alfred Yates, three ordinary seamen and three stokers. Also on board the pinnace were Brownrigg's Goanese steward, his writer and an Arab interpreter. It was Brownrigg's intention to make a tour of inspection of the cutters on patrol off Zanzibar, and to visit the various stores depots on the outlying islands.

On 3 December the pinnace was some 24 miles north of Zanzibar and negotiating the narrow Kokota gap, which runs between the islands of Kokota and Funzi, when a large dhow flying French colours was sighted ahead. Although the dhow had the look of a typical slaver, Brownrigg was reluctant to stop her, as ships of the Royal Navy were forbidden to interfere with French merchant ships, even if they were suspected of being slavers. This prohibition dated back to an incident in 1817, two years after Waterloo, when the French slaver *Louis* was stopped by HMS *Princess Charlotte* off the coast of West Africa, and the ban was still in force.

As *London*'s pinnace approached the dhow, Captain Brownrigg was in the after part with his steward and Yates, who was at the tiller. The rest of the crew were in the fore part, which was separated from aft by a deckhouse. Brownrigg instructed Yates to lay the pinnace alongside the dhow as he wished to examine her papers and to confirm her identity. As she was under the French flag he did not intend to board, and to avoid any misunderstanding he ordered his men to put their rifles away and not to make any threatening moves.

Easing alongside the dhow, Brownrigg took the tiller himself and sent Leading Seaman Yates forward to hook on. The only people visible on the dhow were four men in Arab dress and armed with swords. One of these men, presumably the captain, was waving a roll of papers. There was nothing to indicate that this would be anything but a routine inspection. Then, when Yates was returning aft, he looked down into the dhow, and saw a number of Arabs armed with rifles crouching below the bulwarks.

Yates was unarmed, but he raised the alarm then threw his boathook at the Arabs as they stood up to open fire on the pinnace. He grappled with the first man who tried to board, and fell overboard with him. The Arabs, later estimated to be between fifteen and twenty-five in number, then swarmed aboard the pinnace, firing their guns as they came. The hail of bullets killed one stoker outright, mortally wounded another, and severely wounded two sailors.

Brownrigg and his men had been caught completely unawares. Five of their number were already out of action, and before those remaining could reach their rifles, they were overwhelmed. They saved their lives by jumping overboard into the sea. This left Captain Brownrigg and his Goanese steward isolated in the stern of the pinnace.

Brownrigg snatched up a rifle and shot one of the Arab boarders, but as he struggled to reload he was attacked by several others wielding swords. He reversed his rifle and using it as a club fought off his attackers, knocking two of them overside. But the odds against him were too great. Each time he beat back one assailant, another took his place. A cut across the forehead spurted blood, partially blinding him, then another Arab sword slashed at his hands, severing several fingers and causing him to drop the rifle.

Captain Charles Brownrigg, nurtured in the hard school of the Royal Navy, was a very brave man. Unarmed, completely surrounded by a mob of screaming Arabs, he fought back with his bare hands, always with his face to the foe, and never giving thought to backing away. Finally, weakened by at least twenty sword cuts, he was shot through the heart and fell dead on the deck of his pinnace. He died with the distinction of being the only captain of the Royal Navy to be killed in the war against the African slave traders.

While Brownrigg fought his lonely battle in the stern of the pinnace, Leading Stoker William Venning was treading water astern supporting the wounded Ordinary Seaman Thomas Bishop. Venning, with blood pouring from a head wound, managed to get Bishop into the dinghy towing astern of the pinnace. Unfortunately, the Arabs had witnessed the rescue attempt, and pulled the dinghy back alongside. They hacked the injured Bishop to death.

Three survivors of the massacre, Leading Seaman Alfred Yates, Ordinary Seaman William Colliston and Able Seaman Samuel Massey were still in the water close to the pinnace, Massey wounded and being supported by the others. They would no doubt have suffered the same fate as the unfortunate Bishop, had not the Arabs, in a frenzied attack on the furnishings of the pinnace, hit the boiler safety valve, causing it to lift and send a great gush of scalding steam into the air. Believing they had released some avenging demon, the Arabs retreated back aboard their dhow and made off.

Yates, Colliston and Massey were able to swim the 700 yards to the island of Pemba, meanwhile Leading Stoker Venning had reboarded the pinnace and raised steam again. He picked the three men up off the beach and set course for Zanzibar.

The inspection tour by *London*'s pinnace, which should have been routine and without incident, had gone disastrously wrong, perhaps because those on board had not been sufficiently alert. Four men, Captain Charles Brownrigg, Ordinary Seaman Thomas Bishop, Stoker Richard Monkley, and Brownrigg's writer, John Aess, had lost their lives, while four others were badly wounded.

The incident, particularly the murder of Captain Brownrigg, caused consternation in Zanzibar, and reprisals were demanded. The dhow in question was captured a few days later by a cutter commanded by Lieutenant Lloyd Mathews. Eight Arabs were still on board, among them its captain, who had lost both legs in the fight. He died after confessing to the attack on the pinnace. Whether there had been any slaves on board the dhow is not known, but even if not, it seems almost certain that she was in the trade.

While *London* was stationed at Zanzibar her boats kept the surrounding waters relatively free of the slave trading dhows, but her condition was deteriorating ever more rapidly. Finally, in March of 1884, her hull had become so rotten that she was in danger of sinking at her anchorage, and at the end of the month the Admiralty deemed that she was no longer worth keeping in service. She was decommissioned and towed to Bombay, where she was broken up. Her demise left the East African Squadron without a permanent base in Zanzibar, and her boats were sorely missed.

By this time all European nations had joined ranks with Britain and actively outlawed the trading and carriage of slaves; only the Arabs still persisted. They were the first in the field, and they intended to be the last. It might be said that Arabia, hanging on to the coat tails of Europe's Industrial Revolution, was at long last moving into the 19th century. The coffee plantations of the Yemen were expanding to meet a growing demand, as were the pearl fisheries and date gardens of the Persian Gulf, while there was an increasing need for labour in the Red Sea ports and the sheikhdom of Oman. As the Arabs were essentially nomads, and not given to labouring, it was estimated that around 7000 slaves a year were required to sustain the economy of the Arabian peninsula.

180

With Zanzibar made untenable for the slaving dhows by the vigilance of the Royal Navy, the overland route was being used almost exclusively by the Arab slave traders. At the hub of their activities was a base they had established at Tabora, between Lake Tanganyika and Lake Nyasa. Among those involved was Tippoo Tib, who in 1880 had declared himself Sultan of Nkonde. Tib and his fellow traders had gathered around them large bands of armed followers, and were terrorising British merchants settled in the area. The British armed themselves, and open warfare broke out between the two sides.

The British government was reluctant to come to the aid of the merchants until, a few months later, the Portuguese in Mozambique, seeing an opportunity to acquire more land, sent a military expedition into Nyasaland. London could no longer turn a blind eye, and in 1891 Nyasaland was declared a British Protectorate. The Portuguese were shown the door.

Once British rule was established in the interior of East Africa, an armed campaign was mounted against the Arab slave traders, which in 1895 resulted in their defeat and the execution of their leaders. A trickle of slaves continued to find its way north from the lakes until, in 1898, the last sad procession was caught 100 miles west of Lake Nyasa, the slaves freed, and their captors slain.

Further north a similar pattern was emerging. In 1889 the German government declared a protectorate over an area stretching from the borders of Mozambique to Kilimanjaro, and German East Africa was born. With German rule came, in due course, an end to the slave trade in the protectorate. Uganda followed suit, becoming a British protectorate in 1895, and so centuries of enslavement of the peoples of Central Africa by the Arabs were at last brought to an end by the introduction of European colonial rule.

Organised slave trading on a large scale lived on only in the Upper Nile basin, in Africa's largest country, the Sudan. Sure in the belief that it was their God-given right, the Moslem Arabs of the north mounted regular raids on their black Christian brothers in the south. They then used the waters of the Nile to transport them in chains to Khartoum, and subsequently north to the Mediterranean coast, or east to the Red Sea and so to Arabia and a life of slavery.

General Charles Gordon – the 'Chinese Gordon' of legend – who led the fight against the forces of the Mahdi, had witnessed the work of the Arab slave traders at first hand. He wrote: 'You can scarcely conceive the misery of these poor slaves...No one who has a mother or sisters or children could be callous to the intense human suffering which these poor wretches undergo...I declare, if I could stop this traffic, I would willingly be shot this night.'

Gordon died in the storming of Khartoum in January 1885, after which the Sudan was abandoned to Moslem rule. A bloodbath resulted, in which millions of black Sudanese were murdered. One of Gordon's lieutenants, Slatin Pasha, who was a prisoner of the Moslems, wrote:

> After the defeat of the Shilluks, Zeki Tummal packed thousands of these wretched creatures into the small barges used for the transport of his troops and dispatched them to Omdurman. Hundreds died from suffocation and overcrowding on the journey; and on the arrival of the remnant, the Khalifa appropriated most of the young men as recruits for his bodyguard, whilst the women and young girls were sold by public auction which lasted several days...Hundreds fell ill; and for these poor wretches it was impossible to find purchasers. Wearily they dragged their bodies to the river bank where they died; and as nobody would take the trouble to bury them, the corpses were pushed into the river and swept away.

Gordon's death was avenged in August 1898 when the Khalifa, who succeeded the Mahdi, was roundly defeated at Omdurman by a combined Anglo-Egyptian force under General Kitchener. Sudan then came under a mandate, to be jointly ruled by Britain and Egypt. In reality, the British were firmly in control, the administration and the military being in their hands. From then on, except for the occasional attempts by Arab bands to smuggle small numbers of slaves across the Red Sea, slave trading in the Sudan was at an end.

It had taken all of ninety years, but thanks to the persistence of the British Government and the valiant work of the Royal Navy, Africa had at last rid itself of the evil of slave trading. As for the casualties suffered by the Navy in this long campaign, it is difficult to arrive at an accurate figure; wars being fought in other theatres clouded the issue. But a conservative estimate is believed to be in the region of 2000, with ten times as many again being invalided out of the service. The great majority of these casualties came not in action, but were the result of those dreadful scourges of Africa, malaria, yellow fever, dysentery and heat exhaustion.

Epilogue

Commodore William Jones

Sacred to the memory of Commodore William Jones late Commanding Her Majesty's Ship Penelope on the West Coast of Africa where by his judicious arrangements 115 slave vessels were captured and 6738 human beings were released from slavery between 1st April 1844 and 12th March 1846. Unwilling to relinquish his labours until the energies of life were exhausted he returned to Spithead on the 8th but to die in this Hospital on the 24th May 1846 aged 54 years. Intelligence zeal and perseverance marked the course of his active life and in his last hours his spirit was sustained and comforted by that Christian faith and hope which had informed and animated a mind ever earnestly devoted to the services of his Country and to the kind offices of friendship and humanity.

Memorial at Haslar Hospital, Gosport, Hampshire.

William Jones was typical of the men of the Royal Navy's African Squadron who served and died that Africans taken into slavery might live in freedom. Today, 200 years after the abolition of the slave trade by the British Parliament, his memory is drowned by the loud clamour of the nation's politically correct brigade for Britons to go down on their knees and apologise for their country's role in the slave trade. And no doubt this is what they will do, led by that very Parliament which two centuries ago so bravely defied the rest of the world and showed that no man has the right to hold another in bondage.

The records are incomplete, but it is estimated that in the 18th and 19th centuries some 11 million slaves were taken out of Africa and transported across the Atlantic to the Indies and the Americas. Another 2 million probably went north through Zanzibar and overland in East Africa in the same period. Tens of thousands of others died on the march to the coast and in the barracoons. It was a monstrous trade, and no other country, no other Navy would have had either the will or the ability to put an end to it. Other countries, notably the United States of America and France, did form squadrons to fight the slave trade, but their commitment was questionable and their contribution all but negligible.

The Royal Navy was the only significant player for much of the long campaign, committing as many as thirty ships and over 4000 men for much of the time to hunting down the slave traders. With thousands of miles of coastline, indented by countless hiding places, to watch it all was a hopeless task. At best, no more than one in four of the ships suspected of slaving was being caught. Foreign Office figures for the years 1840 to 1848 reported 444,006 slaves exported from Africa, of which only 31,180 – a mere 7 per cent – were freed by the African Squadron. The cost of this campaign to the British Exchequer was around three-quarters of a million pounds sterling a year, or £36 million in today's money. For the men who manned the ships of the Squadron, the bill was a grim reminder of the magnitude of the task they had undertaken. In any one year, on average, 5 per cent of the men involved would be expected to die on the coast, while another 10 per cent were invalided home, badly injured or too sick to survive in Africa any longer. In his book, *A History of European Morals* (1869) W.H. Lecky stated: 'The weary, unostentatious, and inglorious crusade of England against slavery may probably be regarded as among the three or four virtuous pages comprised in the history of nations.'

There were those, France and America being the most vociferous, who accused Britain of waging the campaign to stamp out the slave trade purely to prove that Britannia still ruled the waves. Given that the campaign cost the British nation a total of some £40 million (equivalent to £2 billion today) and the lives of 2000 seamen, the accusation carries little weight. Those same people also suggested that the trade was not in fact ended by the efforts of the Royal Navy, but more by the American Civil War of 1861-65, which resulted in the abolition of slavery in North America and the freeing of four million slaves in the South. Cuba and Brazil followed suit – albeit twenty years later – and the main markets thus ceased to exist. It may well be that the resolve of the British Parliament and the work of the African Squadron only acted as catalysts in the demise of slavery, but without their efforts Africans would have been condemned to live in servitude for many more years to come.

The abolition of the slave trade led to a scramble for empires in Africa. Britain, France, Germany, Belgium, Spain and Portugal were all eager to carve out a share of this great continent. Missionaries and merchants were followed by agriculturalists, geologists and administrators; treaties were signed with local rulers, territories were annexed, and in place of slaves Africa began to export cocoa, coffee, timber, palm oil, cotton, ground-nuts and minerals, all very much in demand in the West. Under colonial rule Africa prospered and lived in peace for the next hundred years. Africans may have been exploited, but they were not enslaved.

Weary and financially embarrassed after the Second World War, the countries of the West that had held sway in Africa secretly welcomed the 'wind of change' blowing through the continent. 'Independence' was the buzzword of the 1950s and '60s, and one by one the colonies were allowed to go their own way. Almost without exception they had stable economies and the basics of democracy in place; their newly elected governments had only to continue on the course set by their erstwhile colonial masters to progress to full nationhood.

Alas, Africa's way was not that of Europe. In 1869 William Cope Devereux had written:

> Thinking over the state of the people on this coast in reference to the slave trade I came to the conclusion that it might be superseded by legitimate commerce; and that to accomplish this the land must be cultivated to hold the negro to his own soil, and by free labour. But it has been proved in the West Indies and elsewhere that left to himself the negro will work

186

only sufficient to supply his own few wants, and must be actually compelled to work, which after all is slavery although it might take a very mild form and be made instrumental in promoting his own welfare and that of his country to future generations.'

Today Devereux's words would be considered unacceptably racist, but his assessment was to prove correct when the African states gained independence from white rule a century later. In those countries where the Europeans stayed on for a few years, serving in subordinate roles to their new black masters, there was order and progress. But then, when corruption in high places began to empty the coffers, and the popular demand was for the white man to go, he went. The collapse followed quickly, and much of Africa moved from independence and relative prosperity to living on handouts from the West.

The story of Zimbabwe – once Southern Rhodesia – typifies the end of the African dream. This is a country rich in minerals, once the leading producer of the highest grade asbestos, with chrome, nickel and iron ores in abundance and coal mines with a capacity of 6 million tons a year. With Europeans at the helm, the Rhodesian economy flourished. Roads and railways were built, factories opened, and tobacco, wheat, maize, sugar and cotton were farmed on a large scale. Completely self-sufficient in food, the country lived by her exports, and lived well. She was one of Africa's success stories.

The transition to independence in 1953 as part of the Central African Federation went smoothly, and with the whites still in control Rhodesia continued to flourish economically for another twenty-six years despite the sanctions imposed on it in the 1960s and '70s. Then came black majority rule. The whites were kicked out, and under the direction of its president-for-life, Robert Mugabe, Zimbabwe went into steep decline. Today, unable even to feed itself, with inflation at 2000 per cent, and an unchecked epidemic of Aids tearing great chunks out of its population, Zimbabwe is entirely dependent on foreign aid.

Much of sub-Saharan Africa has joined, or is in the process of joining, Zimbabwe in the world's poorhouse. Nigeria, which has vast oil reserves in the Niger Delta, has earned herself the distinction of being branded the most corrupt nation on the face of the

Earth. Sudan, the largest country in Africa, has been torn by a bitter civil war between the Muslim north and the Christian south on and off for almost fifty years, resulting in the deaths of up to 2 million people. The list is endless. Countries once prosperous and at peace cannot hope to survive without their begging bowls being regularly filled by the West.

And as self-impoverished Africa slips back into the abyss of the dark ages, the slave trade has returned. The Anti-Slavery Society reports:

> Recently, we have seen the revival of the once thriving slave routes across West Africa, after a lapse of 25 years. Slavers have reappeared following the old slave trade routes, except that trucks, jeeps and modern four-wheel drive vehicles and, on occasions, aircraft, have replaced the camels. The slavers often carry mobile phones.
>
> Some things, however, have not changed. Cunning, deceit, the use of drugs to subdue the children and the whip still remain part of the essential equipment of the professional slaver.
>
> The trade involves most states in sub-Saharan Africa.
>
> The children are kidnapped or purchased for $20-$70 each by slavers in poorer states, such as Benin and Togo, and sold into slavery in sex dens or as unpaid domestic servants for $350 each in wealthier oil-rich states, such as Nigeria and Gabon.

There is a regular market for slaves in the old French colony of Ivory Coast, which has extensive cocoa plantations. Teenage slaves are on sale in the capital Abidjan for as little as $40 a head. As of old, they are picked up clandestinely in the Bight of Benin and transported in 21st century slave ships one of which was the Nigerian-registered *Etireno*. In April 2001 this ancient rust-bucket called at Douala in Cameroon, and was found to have 250 children on board. The local authorities suspected that these were child slaves on their way to the Ivory Coast, but before they were able to act, the *Etireno* had slipped away to sea. She tried to enter two or three other ports, but by this time the story had reached the international press, and was splashed across the world. The *Etireno* disappeared off the radar screens, and it is not known what happened to her and her cargo of children.

Child slavery is now rife in Africa. According to the United Nations Children's Fund, UNICEF, more than 15,000 children are working in the plantations of Ivory Coast alone. Many of these boys and girls, some as young as seven, are sold into slavery by their own parents for as little as $30 in the belief that they will be given a good education and well paid work. Others are kidnapped or handed over by orphanages that can no longer afford to keep them. As the African way of life produces so many children who have no future, the slave traders never go short.

Anti-Slavery International has recently reported that slavery is now practised in the Sudan on a large scale. Amnesty International has produced evidence that government militiamen often raid the remote mountain regions for young girls, who are then sold into slavery in the cities. In this war-torn country, with millions dependent on food aid, anything is acceptable.

On Zanzibar Island, where Sultan Seyyid Said once ruled and the slave markets thrived, there is a new commodity on the streets. Italian drug dealers have turned the Spice Island into a base for heroin smuggling. In the old harbour, in the place of Suri dhows awaiting their illicit cargoes, sleek powerboats are moored ready to rendezvous off shore with container ships coming from the Far East. And who is to stop them? The cruisers of the African Squadron are only a very distant memory, and the corrupt officials who run the island turn a blind eye to the parcels of drugs changing hands.

Africa, crippled by debt, and dying of Aids, staggers from crisis to crisis, urged on by naïve foreign politicians and publicity-seeking celebrities who think they can cure this continent's grievous ills by throwing money at them.

Bibliography

Bell, Christopher, *Portugal and the Quest for the Indies*, Constable, 1974

Bready, J. Wesley, *England Before and After Wesley*, Hodder & Stoughton, 1937

Coates, Marion, *Sea Sequel*, Nonesuch Press, 1934

Cope Devereaux, W., *A Cruise in the Gorgon*, Dawsons of Pall Mall, 1968

Coupland, R., *The British Anti-Slavery Movement*, Thornton Butterworth, 1933

Coupland, R., *Exploitation of East Africa 1856-1890*, Faber & Faber, 1939

Everett, Susanne, *History of Slavery*, Bison Books, 1978

Gerzina, Gretchen, *Black England – Life Before Emancipation*, John Murray, 1995

Hill, J.R., *Oxford Illustrated History of the Royal Navy*, Oxford University Press, 1995

Howells, Raymond, *The Royal Navy and the Slave Trade*, Croom Helm Ltd., 1987

Hydrographer to the Navy, *Africa Pilot Vol. 1*, 1967

Hydrographer to the Navy, *Africa Pilot Vol. 3*, 1967

Keble Chatterton, E., *Valiant Sailormen*, Hurst & Blackett, 1936

Kennedy, Sister Jean de Chantal, *Bermuda's Sailors of Fortune*, Bermuda Historical Society, 1963

Lewis, Roy & Foy, Yvonne, *The British in Africa*, Weidenfeld & Nicolson, 1971

Lloyd, Christopher, *The Navy and the Slave Trade*, Longmans Green & Co., 1949

Lloyd, Christopher, *The British Seaman*, Collins, 1968

Mannix, Daniel P. & Cowley, Malcolm, *Black Cargoes*, Longmans, Green & Co., 1963

McCarthy, Justin, *A Short History of Our Own Times*, Chatto & Windus, 1908

Padfield, Peter, *Rule Britannia*, Pimlico, 1981

Price, Anthony, *The Eyes of the Fleet*, Hutchinson, 1990

Ransford, Oliver, *The Slave Trade*, John Murray, 1871

Royale, Trevor, *Winds of Change*, John Murray, 1996

Sillery, David, *Africa – A Social Geography*, Duckworth, 1961

Sulivan, Captain G.J., RN, *Dhow Chasing in Zanzibar Waters*, The Gallery Publications, 2003

Tattersfield, Nigel, *The Forgotten Trade*, Jonathan Cape, 1991

Thomas, Hugh, *The Slave Trade*, Picador, 1997

Walvin, James, *Black Ivory – A History of British Slavery*, Harper Collins, 1992

Ward, W.E.F., *The Royal Navy and the Slavers*, George Allen & Unwin, 1969

Williams, Basil, *The British Empire*, Thornton Butterworth Ltd., 1928

Winton, John, *The Victoria Cross at Sea*, Michael Joseph, 1978

Other Sources

National Archives, National Maritime Museum, Admiralty Library, Royal Naval Museum, Naval Maritime Museum, Royal Marine Museum, Navy Records Society, US Department of Navy, Merseyside Maritime Museum, Anti-Slavery Society,
The Times, The Monmouthshire Merlin & South Wales Advertiser, The Mariner's Mirror, The Nautical Magazine

Index

195

196